THE P&O LIN

C000228163

and
PRINCESS CRUISES

Carola Ingall

A Celebration in Pictures of
THE PENINSULAR & ORIENTAL STEAM NAVIGATION COMPANY

SHIP PICTORIAL PUBLICATIONS
1997

Cover: CANBERRA in the Falklands by Richard Ward. By kind permission of Noel Tatt Ltd.

For John

First published 1997 by Ship Pictorial Publications
The Cabinet, High Street, Coltishall, Norfolk NR12 7AA

© Carola Ingall 1997

British Library Cataloguing in Publication Data
Ingall, Carola
    The P&O Line and Princess Cruises:
    A Celebration in Pictures of
    the Peninsular & Oriental Steam Navigation Company
    I. Title
    ....

    ISBN 0 9516038 6 8

Ship Pictorial Series:
S.P.P.1   The Cunard Line (Peter W. Woolley & Terry Moore)
S.P.P.2   The Union-Castle Line (Alan S. Mallett)
S.P.P.3   The White Star Line (Paul Louden-Brown)
S.P.P.4   Shaw Savill & Albion (Richard de Kerbrech)
S.P.P.5   The Holland America Line (Peter Kohler)
S.P.P.7   The P&O Line (Carola Ingall)

Typeset by Carola Ingall

Printed and bound by Page Bros (Norwich) Ltd

INTRODUCTION AND ACKNOWLEDGMENTS

The P&O, being Britain's oldest surviving shipping company, has been extensively documented, and I am not trying to present a brand new history of the Company or its ships. Details of many interesting publications appear in the Select Bibliography.

Born in India before the Second World War, I had the "feel" of the Company long before I knew anything at all about its origin or history. My parents and grand-parents (probably even my great grandfather, who went to India and Egypt) travelled P&O, and another antecedent suffered a most uncomfortable voyage to the Crimea as one of Florence Nightingale's nurses, in the VECTIS. My own "first ship" (I wish I could remember her) was RAJPUTANA in 1938, and once I was grown up all I wanted was to go to sea with P&O. After 3 years working at Head Office—the glorious 122 Leadenhall Street—my ambition was rewarded and I joined STRATHMORE as a "Seagoing Stenographer," reaching the dizzy heights of Woman Assistant Purser before I foolishly left the sea (temporarily as I believed at the time) to work in Hong Kong. But P&O is still "my Company" and I have retained my interest and connections with my former shore and ship-mates ever since.

I am greatly indebted to Stephen Rabson, P&O Group Librarian, for his advice and helpful interest, as well as his permission to consult Company records and reproduce Company photographs, also his assistant Lyn Palmer. Bill Williams, a dear friend whom I've known since I worked for him at "122", has been wonderful, in reading drafts and making extremely helpful comments and suggestions, also Peter "Dai" Evans; I'd like to thank my other P&O and shipping-mad friends for their loans and gifts of P&O material and artefacts; finally and certainly not least, I am so grateful to John Parratt, for allowing me free rein with his office and equipment in the evenings, at weekends and quite often during the day as well! Most of the pictures originate from postcards and photographs in my own collection or kindly given or loaned by the Company, although there are some depictions of earlier vessels where no photographs, and certainly no postcards, exist. All the items of ephemera portrayed are in my collection. With regard to copyright, I have done my best to obtain permission from copyright holders and, where contact has been made, this has been given wholeheartedly. However, particularly in the case of some of the older pictures, my letters have been returned marked "unknown" or else they are still falling to the bottom of the well and I have yet to hear the "plop". In any case where I may have used a picture without obtaining specific permission, I can only ask that the copyright holder accepts these notes as my personal acknowledgment and thanks.

With such a long history, and such a huge number of ships owned by the Company over nearly 160 years, there will be many omissions. The most immediately apparent will perhaps be the ships of the Orient Line which became part of the P&O fleet with the formation of P&O Orient Lines in 1960. I have done this deliberately, in the hope that Orient liners may perhaps have a similar publication of their own in due course. This also applies to UGANDA and the British India S.N. Company. I hope this book will give a flavour of a mighty Company which has coloured my life, and that of countless others—long may it continue to do so.

CAROLA INGALL
Alton, August 1997

PENINSULAR AND ORIENTAL STEAM NAVIGATION COMPANY

A BRIEF HISTORY
THE PENINSULAR & ORIENTAL STEAM NAVIGATION COMPANY

The Peninsular and Oriental Steam Navigation Company, better known just by the initials P & O: Everyone's heard the name, but many people have no real idea of what it means or how it originated. Today, it means shopping centres, building developments, containers, road tankers, exhibition centres and—ships.

This Company began at a time of huge change and upheaval; the Industrial Revolution was well under way, but until the early part of the 19th century, transport had not been much affected. Now, a new method of propulsion was gripping the imagination of the young and far-seeing: Steam! From early experiment and development of steam-propelled vessels in Scotland, France and America, the momentum of change from sail to steam was gathering pace, and P&O, probably the oldest and certainly the greatest British shipping Company still in operation has its origin in this exciting, risky, daring time.

The origins of the P&O lie in the efforts primarily of two young men in pre-Victorian London. Perhaps Arthur Anderson's story is the more romantic of the two—his life is certainly better documented. He came from very humble origins, born in Shetland in 1792. He was lucky in his parents and his schoolmaster, who taught him well and encouraged him in his desire to learn as much as he could. Initially, Anderson served in The Royal Navy, as a clerk, but after the Napoleonic Wars, he was paid off in Portsmouth with so little money, that he had to walk to London. He was looking for work, and met Brodie McGhie Willcox, who took him on as a clerk in his City shipbroking office. All we know of Willcox is that he was born in Newcastle (not Ostend, as previously believed) in 1785. By 1823, Willcox and Anderson were working in partnership. Anderson had gained valuable knowledge and experience of ships and had travelled widely with the Navy. He and Willcox developed their business from purely shipbroking, to operating ships on their own account, particularly to the Spanish and Portuguese peninsula. They started with small, chartered sailing vessels, but soon demonstrated the advantages of steam with their introduction of early steam-propelled vessels, also chartered to begin with.

At about this time, both Spain and Portugal were plunged into revolution against their respective Royal families. Luckily as it turned out, Willcox and Anderson chose to support the Royalists, gaining prestige and some influence when the rightful heirs were restored in both cases.

It is from this period that the Company flag originates—no modern "logo" but the house colours of the Portuguese and Spanish royal families: blue and white for Portugal and red and yellow for Spain: "Blue to the yard, Red to the fly, Yellow below and White on high." It is interesting that the flag was originally a pennant, with Yellow above.

A milestone in the affairs of Willcox and Anderson was 1826, when they became London agents for the Dublin and London Steam Packet Company, of which Captain Richard Bourne was Managing Director. The Spanish Minister in London was keen to have a regular service to the Iberian peninsula, and the Dublin steamers were chosen to provide it, with Willcox and Anderson managing the fleet. Their knowledge of the route, combined with Richard Bourne's ships, led to the formation, in 1835, of the Peninsular Steam Navigation Company, with the object of trading to and from Spain and Portugal. An initial attempt to "float" Peninsular Steam had failed in 1834, but in 1835 the first advertised sailings took place, WILLIAM FAWCETT, chartered from Richard Bourne, being traditionally regarded as the Company's first ship.

Change was in the air for the carriage of mails by sea. For many years, the mail "packet" ships had the monopoly, but they were totally unsatisfactory and unreliable. They sailed according to weather and personal inclination, and frequently "lost" the mails. Sometimes the Captains didn't even sail with their ships, but stayed warm and safe at home, while their crews, often inexperienced and/or dishonest, made the voyage. The mail might arrive safely—or it might not. It was decided that the Admiralty should take over responsibility for carriage of the mails from 1836, but there was still the problem of regularity of departure, as of course all Her Majesty's ships were propelled by sail alone, and the Admiralty was dead set against any change.

It was clear to Willcox and Anderson that with steam propulsion, regular schedules could be advertised and achieved. By this time, enthusiasm for steamships was widespread and companies were springing up all over the place, hoping for good fortune and success. It was clear that a mail contract was vital to the Company's prospects for the future, and in 1837 the directors were successful in persuading the Admiralty to award them the contract to carry mails to Spain and Portugal. This is the generally accepted date for the founding of the Company.

The Company prospered, and established a reputation for punctuality and reliability, although of course there were setbacks and difficulties—one in particular could have spoilt everything at the outset: On the first mail contract voyage in 1837, the newly-built DON JUAN on her maiden voyage, with Arthur Anderson aboard, sank on her way home as a result of striking a rock near Gibraltar. Captain Engledue, who later became a director of the company, was quite surprisingly exonerated from blame, as the fog was totally unexpected and impenetrable. Fortunately, the mails were saved (plus all the passengers, crew and the specie), and all was well—apart from the loss of the ship of course—but it must have been a nasty moment.

By 1840, the Directors had set their sights further afield and, after negotiations with the Admiralty, were awarded a contract to carry the mails to Alexandria, for onward transmission to the East. A condition was that the service be extended to India within 2 years. This was achieved. Further funds were needed and in order to raise £1 million with limited liability, incorporation by charter was necessary—this was before the Companies Act. Thus came into being The Peninsular and Oriental Steam Navigation Company, incorporated by Royal Charter. This remains the full title of today's well-known, abbreviated "P&O."

Provided with this firm foundation for progress and expansion, Willcox, Anderson and their colleagues rapidly built up their Company, extending its operations by the middle of the century to Calcutta, Bombay, Ceylon, Singapore, Hong Kong and Shanghai, as well as routes within the Mediterranean. By 1852, they were running to Australia, but were no longer serving the Iberian Peninsula, the basis from which their success originated.

But there was still the problem of the neck of land joining Africa with Asia, and how it was to be crossed. To solve this difficulty, the Company developed and improved on an existing system. It was complicated and really extremely efficient, albeit rather uncomfortable: passengers disembarked at Alexandria, went by riverboat in two stages to Cairo, and, until a railway was built, travelled across the desert to Suez by horse-drawn "stage coach", with rest stations provided by the

Company en route. The Egyptian Government nationalised the Transit in 1845, which did not improve efficiency. This arrangement lasted for many years, continuing for a while even after the building and inauguration of the Suez Canal in 1869. The P & O were untypically wrong-footed over this, believing it would not be a success. Huge investment had been made in the infrastructure of the overland route and it was hard to realise that the opening of the Suez Canal had virtually rendered all of this worthless.

Also, they thought their existing two separate fleets, one for the temperate zone as far as Alexandria and the other for east of Suez, would be adequate. They were wrong. The company began to be left behind in the commercial competition for success on the route to the East, being undercut by new companies whose vessels were suitable to cover the whole voyage. Even when the P&O did start to use the Canal, the Post Office (responsible for mail contracts since 1861) still insisted that the mails be carried overland, sometimes discharged from and re-loaded in the same vessel. This was the situation, in part at any rate, until 1886. Willcox had died in 1862 and Anderson in 1868. Problems of route and suitability of vessels were gradually overcome and the Company they had founded was by then a symbol of Victorian imperial success and influence. Larger and faster ships, more suitable to cover the whole voyage from Britain and through the Suez Canal, were built and technological innovation was cautiously introduced, nearly always when it had already been proved by someone else. Shore stations, coal depots, docks and workshops were established throughout the Company's routes, and a reputation for comfort, safety and good living aboard the Company's vessels, though the provision of free wine and spirits came to an end in the 1870s!

Apart from the mails, cargo carried in the Company's vessels consisted originally of valuable items such as gold and silver bullion, silk and indigo. Competition on its traditional routes, particularly after the opening of the Suez Canal, was not restricted to passengers, and the Company had to develop its cargo operations, not only to widen the variety of cargo carried, but to introduce more competitive rates. Carriage of the mails from 1836, with punctuality and safe delivery, however, remained the first priority, on occasion even above the requirements of passengers although, in the event of disaster, the passengers just about came first!

Thomas Sutherland, who started his career with P&O as a clerk in the London Office and later in Hong Kong, became Managing Director in 1872 and Chairman in 1881. He was the towering personality of the Company until the First World War, and took the responsibility for rebuilding the fleet to meet the new circumstances. During this time, the P&O was increasingly subject to competition on all its routes, and there were many new developments, including the establishment of the first freight conferences for the regulation between carriers of routes, schedules and cargo rates.

The Company's home port in Britain, which had been Southampton for forty years since 1841, reverted to London, and since the opening of the Suez Canal, it became much more convenient to repair, maintain, and supply the ships in Britain, although the tradition of employing at least part of the crews from the Indian Sub-continent continued, and indeed does so to this day in some vessels.

In 1910, P&O acquired the Blue Anchor Line, owners of the ill-fated WARATAH, enabling them to enter the market in economy passages to Australia via the Cape. Known as the P&O Branch Service, it lasted until 1936.

Lord Inchcape, another almost legendary figure in the Company's history and formerly Chairman of the British India

Steam Navigation Company, took over Chairmanship of both companies after their merger in 1914. This was the start of the P&O Group. Lord Inchcape foresaw a serious shortage of post-war tonnage, and even while the War continued, he began to buy other shipping companies. First was the New Zealand Shipping Company in 1916; the Union Steamship Company of New Zealand, with the Hain and Nourse Lines, followed in 1917; a 51% interest in the Orient Line was acquired in 1919 and the General Steam Navigation Company was purchased in 1920. All (apart from the Orient Line, which was merged in 1960) maintained their separate identities and individual operations until 1971 when the 100 or so companies within the group were reorganised into Divisions according to their type of operation. These divisions were later dismantled and individual trading companies re-established within the Group.

So far, P&O's huge contribution to various war efforts has not been mentioned. This first arose at the very beginning of the Company's operations, when an artillery Company was taken by ORIENTAL to Malta in 1840, and has continued up to the Falklands in 1982. In 1854 at the time of the Crimean War, several of the Company's vessels were either chartered by or sold to the Government, and in the Egyptian crisis of the 1880's TANJORE served as a refugee ship off Alexandria—she also took General Gordon as a passenger from Brindisi to Port Said on his fateful last journey to Egypt. Huge losses were sustained by the P&O in both World Wars. Casualties were heavy among ships which continued to ply their normal trade as cargo vessels in the war effort, and many losses also occurred amongst those employed as Armed Merchant Cruisers and Troopships. At the time of the first World War, the P&O Group owned about 300 vessels, of which 56 were lost and in the second, 182 ships were destroyed out of a total Group ownership of 460. The reputation of the Company's ships was unparalleled, and there are many well documented examples of valour and self-sacrifice among ships' companies. In addition to providing its own vessels for Government use, the Company has from time to time managed and operated Troopships on behalf of HM Government.

Between the wars, losses were replaced and the fleet continued to be expanded and modernised. Cruising had tentatively been started as far back as 1844, when the Company invited the novelist William Thackeray to make a trip in the Mediterranean, travelling in three of the Company's ships. In 1904 the Company's vessel ROME was fitted out for cruising, having been renamed VECTIS. After the First World War, the popularity of cruising increased, although the ships employed were all built for passenger and cargo trade on traditional routes, even the Company's "Jewel in the Crown" VICEROY OF INDIA, and the white-liveried STRATHs, with buff-coloured funnels, which came on the scene in the 1930s. Until then, with a few exceptions, the P&O ships were painted black, with a white line round the hull, and stone-coloured upperworks.

But once again, developing prosperity and future hopes of the Company were to be brought to a halt by armed conflict. Again a huge contribution was exacted on behalf of Great Britain, in terms of lives lost and tonnage sunk during the Second World War. Many famous names disappeared, including the lovely VICEROY and STRATHALLAN, latest of the STRATHs. RAWALPINDI's name went down in history for her gallant and suicidal confrontation of the German Battlecruisers GNEISENAU and SCHARNHORST, and there were many, many more instances of supreme bravery by officers and crew.

When the War ended, return to peacetime operation was painful and slow, due to delays in the return from Government services of the ships which had survived the War. This was largely due to shortages in labour and materials, and there was a lack of funds to pay for new tonnage to replace that which had been lost; not until almost 1950 were the last of the pre-War passenger ships returned to Company service, and the cargo fleet restored to its pre-War size. Under the Chairmanship of Sir William Currie, the first new passenger liners were HIMALAYA and CHUSAN, followed in 1954 by ARCADIA and IBERIA. Several of the older ships, such as MOOLTAN, MALOJA, STRATHAIRD and STRATHNAVER were converted to one-class, and provided a large share of the berths demanded by the post-War emigrant exodus to Australia, as did the Tourist class accommodation in those vessels which continued to provide two-class travel. Several general cargo vessels were equipped to carry up to 12 passengers, and the Company began the wider development of its shipping operations, by entering the tanker market.

Cruising began once more, with CHUSAN in 1950, and provided significant income both in the traditional areas of the northern hemisphere, and also from time to time based on Australian ports. In 1954, P&O reinstated its service to Japan and in 1960 extended its services across the Pacific as a result of a merger with the Orient Line. The companies had been connected since 1919, but now a combined identity was formed as "P&O Orient Lines", a name which only lasted for 6 years.

At the same time, two new vessels, the largest passenger liners yet owned by the Company, came into service. In 1960 ORIANA made her maiden voyage in the Orient Line livery of corn-coloured hull and funnel, with white upperworks and green boot-topping, and in 1961, CANBERRA joined the P&O fleet. Shortly, however, all the passenger ships of both fleets were operating as one, in the same white and buff P&O livery, with officers serving in any of them, although the Orient ships continued to be staffed wholly by European crews, and the P&O vessels by the traditional mix of about half the crew from India, Pakistan and Goa.

By this time, the shadow of air travel lay dark across the liner routes for passengers, and containerisation was soon to have a revolutionary effect on the carriage of cargo. The years between the P&O-Orient merger and the 150th Anniversary of the Company's founding in 1987 were to see huge changes in emphasis in the P&O's business. All the pre-War passenger ships had been disposed of, as well as most of the post-War ships, and all the traditional liner voyages were ended by 1973. Those passenger ships remaining were exclusively engaged in the cruise market which had become the only raison d'etre for such vessels.

In 1974 P&O bought Bovis, the housebuilding and construction firm, and in 1983, following the unsuccessful bid for the Company by Trafalgar House, Jeffrey Sterling, now Lord Sterling of Plaistow, became Chairman. Because of the uncertainty of profitability from shipping interests alone, the scope of P&O operations was widened hugely, bringing in many subsidiary companies. The company was already involved in bulk carriers, ferries and road haulage, but the 1985 merger with Sterling Guarantee Trust brought in an even wider variety of concerns, such as property and services, eg exhibition centres and catering (the latter since sold). (P&O) European Ferries were acquired in 1987, being a significant enlargement of a previously minor interest. The Company, already the largest UK ferry operator, and possibly the biggest in the world, announced yet further developments in 1996 by taking over Nedlloyd's half of North Sea Ferries and establishing a joint operation on the short sea Channel services with Stena Line. The P&O's interests continue to expand worldwide, evidenced by their 1996 merger with Nedlloyd, to form P&O Nedlloyd, a new giant in the container trade.

In the meantime, the Falklands War in 1982 caused six vessels belonging to the P&O to become STUFT (Ships Taken Up From Trade). All played a vital part once more, in providing seaborne support for their country in time of conflict. As well as ELK, NORLAND, STRATHEWE and the 50%-owned ANCO CHARGER, they included CANBERRA (The Great White Whale) and the ex-BI educational cruise ship UGANDA. The former acted as a troop carrier, supply ship, replacement unit and forward dressing station, right into the centre of the danger zone, and the latter ("Mother Hen") was the Fleet Hospital Ship. To fill the gap left by the enforced withdrawal of UGANDA from educational cruising in 1982 (she returned very briefly in 1983) the Swan Hellenic Group was acquired by P&O in 1983.

Cruising remains the most glamorous of the P&O's maritime interests. In 1974, the Company bought Princess Cruises, who operated only one ship at the time: ISLAND PRINCESS; PACIFIC PRINCESS was purchased in 1975, followed by the building of ROYAL PRINCESS in 1984. Later, in 1988, P&O took over the four ships of the Sitmar fleet, which became part of the Princess operation based in Los Angeles. Three Sitmar-ordered vessels, later joined the Princess fleet as STAR, CROWN and REGAL PRINCESS, as well as the chartered GOLDEN PRINCESS. ISLAND, PACIFIC, ROYAL and SKY PRINCESSes have British Officers and British registration. The other Princess ships are registered abroad and have retained their Italian flavour, with Italian officers. All the ships have multi-national crew.

SUN PRINCESS (77,000 tons) joined the Princess fleet in December 1995—at the time the largest cruise ship in the world, and the largest to pass through the Panama Canal. She is followed by three sisters, DAWN, SEA and OCEAN PRINCESS. GRAND PRINCESS, at 105,000 tons the largest cruise ship ever built, will come into service in late 1997. These new vessels, with foreign registration, are from the Fincantieri yard in Italy. From time to time, a Princess calls at a UK port—always a welcome occasion to see one of P&O's "expatriates". In 1996 Princess Cruises were awarded the James E. McGuire Safety Award, the world's highest for marine safety, the first time it has been presented to a cruise line. Princess Cruises are the only cruise line which carry a "black box" voyage recorder on every ship, and were three years ahead of the deadline to meet the standards for safety and pollution prevention set by the International Maritime Organisation.

In Britain, based in Southampton and operated by P&O Cruises Ltd, is the only survivor of the 1960's fleet, CANBERRA, (to be withdrawn in 1997 and replaced by STAR PRINCESS renamed ARCADIA), together with the recently re-named VICTORIA (previously SEA PRINCESS, ex Swedish Line KUNGSHOLM 1966), leased by P&O in 1979. Both are British-registered. In April 1995, these ships were joined by the new ORIANA, also of British registry. Clearly a ship of the 90's, she is nevertheless "daughter of CANBERRA" in appearance; As in CANBERRA and VICTORIA, her Officers are British and her crew partly Asian, in keeping with P&O tradition. ORIANA, VICTORIA, ARCADIA and another new ship as yet unnamed are destined to sail, with the Princess fleet, into the 21st Century, proudly bearing the quartered houseflag of the P&O—a living link between those far-off days of early steam travel from Victorian Britain, and the high-tech world of modern journeys for pleasure, but still epitomising the Company's tradition of safety, comfort and service.

ROYAL PRINCESS in an ice-bound river after floating out.

NOTES TO ILLUSTRATIONS

1. All illustrations are taken from the author's collection, or loaned by P&O, except where otherwise noted.
2. Roman numeral(s) following a ship's name indicate the first, second etc. vessel of that name in P&O Line service.
3. Dates following a ship's name indicate the length of time in P&O Line service.
4. The origin of each vessel's name is stated on the right.
5. Brief statistical details of each vessel illustrated are listed in the Index on pages 167–171.
6. Tonnage shown on some illustrations may differ from that shown in the Index. This is due to modifications during a ship's career.
7. The term "class" indicates that the vessel in question is one of several ships of broadly similar design. The term "sister ship(s)" indicates that these vessels were built to the same dimensions, specifications and power and were generally similar but not necessarily identical in appearance and layout.

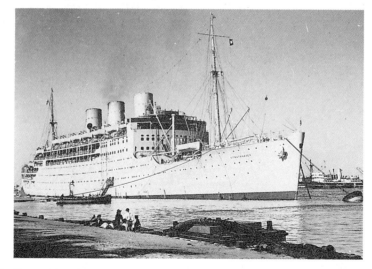

STRATHNAVER refuelling at Port Said.

THE STEAM-SHIP "IBERIA," WITH "CUNNINGHAM'S PATENT TOPSAIL."

IBERIA (I)   Spanish/Portuguese Peninsula

1836/56.   Wooden Paddle Steamer

Built by Curling & Young, Limehouse, the first vessel actually ordered by Willcox and Anderson. Registered in their name until 1841 when she was registered in the name of the Company. 1856 sold to North of Europe Steam Navigation Co, but the sale fell through and she was bought by G. Marks for demolition at Greenwich.

GREAT LIVERPOOL   Lancashire city in England
1840/46.   Wooden Paddle Steamer: Southampton/Alexandria
Built by Humble & Milcrest, Liverpool. The first two-funnelled steamer. Laid down for Trans Atlantic Steamship Company, but bought by P&O whilst on the stocks. She was given the prefix "Great", to distinguish her from the LIVERPOOL already owned by the Company. Homeward bound for Southampton from Alexandria in February 1846 she struck a reef off Cape Finisterre. The Captain managed to beach her on the Spanish coast, but the wreck was looted. Three days later she broke up in a storm with loss of 3 lives. An enquiry held the Captain blameless, but he was so upset he committed suicide by cutting his throat in his hotel room.

EUXINE   Classical name for the Black Sea
1847/1868.   Iron Paddle Steamer
Built by Caird & Co, Greenock. Uneventful career with the Company, but after she was sold to Edward Bates, Liverpool and converted to a sailing ship, she caught fire in the South Atlantic, en route for Aden with a cargo of coal. 23 of the crew reached St Helena in one of the ship's boats and 5 more were picked up by a Dutch ship, but not before they had killed and eaten one of their shipmates.

INDUS (I)   Great river in Pakistan
1847/69.   Iron Paddle Steamer, later Sailing Ship. Southampton/Alexandria then via Cape
Built by Money Wigram & Sons, Blackwall. Laid down as MADRAS. 1852 she was returned to her builders for lengthening, but almost at once caught fire in dry dock, necessitating fitting of new engines, boilers and paddles. Ten years later, she was converted to sail, to act as a supply ship via the Cape of Good Hope, carrying stores and machinery in support of the Company's Indian-based fleet. New engines originally intended for her were fitted to SYRIA. Sold 1869, with an active life of a further 20 years. From 1889 used as a hulk in Zanzibar, finally scuttled off Mombasa in 1894.

FORMOSA (I)   Island now known as Taiwan
1852/70.   Iron Passenger Liner. Purchased for Singapore/Sydney but employed Calcutta/China
Built by Smith & Rodger, Govan as CALEDONIA for Malcomson Brothers, Waterford; bought by the Company after launching and renamed FORMOSA before leaving her builders. 1861 she was chartered by the French Government to serve as a transport between Singapore and Saigon. In 1867 she struck a rock off Ocksen Island and was beached at Amoy, where she was repaired. She was sold in 1870, and various Far Eastern owners are recorded until 1929, since when there are no records of her.

VECTIS (II)   Roman name for the Isle of Wight

1853/65.   Wooden Paddle Steamer, employed Marseilles/Malta

Built by Thomas & Robert White, Cowes, Isle of Wight. In October/November 1854 Florence Nightingale travelled to the
Crimea in this ship, and one of her nurses wrote in her diary of their desperately uncomfortable voyage. A storm, later
famous for its ferocity, struck the ship and hurled tons of icy seawater into the nurses' cabin in the forepart of the vessel.
They were lying on wooden bunks overlaid with straw, which became soaked, while water swirled around the deck at their
feet. Most of them were terribly sick and almost longed to die by the time the weather moderated. Sarah Anne Terrot
records how some of the nurses rushed on deck, pleading with the Captain to "stop the ship", and the kindness of the
Stewardess who looked after them as best she could.   (Photo: Southampton City Museums)

6

HIMALAYA (I)   Highest mountain range in the world, Northern India

1853/54.   Iron Passenger Liner, Southampton/Alexandria mail service

Built by C.J. Mare & Co, Blackwall. The largest ship in the world, her entry into service coincided with a 50% increase in the cost of fuel. She proved really too large for the Company's current requirements, but was ideal for transporting troops to the Crimea. The Government first chartered and, in 1854, bought the ship from the P&O. Describing the passage of the 5th Dragoons to Sebastopol, Sergeant Major Franks gives an interesting account of the trip, from the point of view of a senior NCO, including the Court Martial of a Sergeant for bringing alcohol aboard in Malta. He was acquitted, but only because someone else carried it for him! In 1894 placed in reserve and in 1895 reduced to HM Hulk C60. In this capacity, she lay at Devonport, Chatham and finally Portland, where in 1940 her long career ended violently when she was bombed and sunk by German aircraft.

ALMA

River in the Crimea, scene of a battle in 1854

1855/1859.   Iron Passenger Liner. Suez/Calcutta service

Launched as PERA for the Company, by John Laird, Sons & Co, Birkenhead. Renamed prior to completion, in salute to the British victory at Alma in the Crimea. Employed for her first 18 months as a Troopship to the Crimea. 1855 commenced commercial service. 1859 whilst on passage from Aden to Suez, she was wrecked on a coral reef in the Red Sea, but fortunately there was no loss of life.

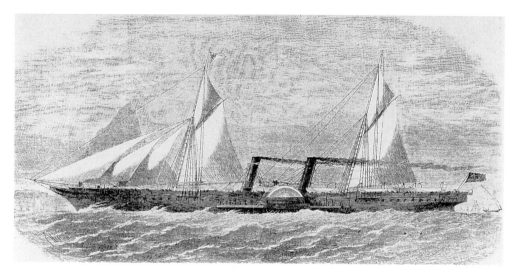

NYANZA (I)   Former name of Lake Victoria in Africa
1864/1873.   Iron Paddle Steamer

The last P&O paddle steamer. Her most interesting period was with her third owner, the Sultan of Zanzibar, who used her as his private yacht, and also to deliver his Crown Tribute to Aden where it was transhipped to P&O vessels for onward carriage to England. In 1889 she was damaged by an unidentified vessel in the Suez Canal, but salvaged and repaired. Sold twice more within Zanzibar; finally broken up in Bombay in 1904.

DECCAN

Plateau in India

1868/1889.   Iron Passenger Liner

In the late seventies, the first P&O ship to run direct to Australia via the Cape on what was advertised as "the cool weather route", but the Company soon reverted to using the Suez Canal. The last P&O ship based on Southampton, before London became the home port in 1881. Employed as a Troopship in the Egyptian Campaign of 1882, and the Egyptian War of 1884/85. Sold in 1889 to Hajee Cassum Joosum, Bombay; finally disappeared without trace off Mauritius—possibly capsized in bad weather due to pump failure and the swelling of sugar cargo in the holds.

ASSAM   North-Eastern state, India

1875/1895.   Iron Passenger Liner, India/Australia and Italy/India services

1873 Built by Caird & Co, Greenock for North German Lloyd as **FELDMARSCHALL MOLKE**. Bought by P&O in 1875. Carried 144 first class and 68 second class passengers; her 'tween decks could if necessary be converted for steerage class, which must have been almost unbearable in the heat of the tropics. 1895 sold to Nippon Yusen Kaisha, renamed **KAIJIO MARU** and broken up in Japan in 1898.

R.M.S. Oceana

Wishing you a Happy. Xmas.

OCEANA   Feminine form of Latin name for the Ocean

1888/1912.   Passenger Liner, designed for Australian service, later employed Indian service

Built by Harland & Wolff Ltd, Belfast. One of 4 vessels, built to celebrate both the Jubilee of Queen Victoria and that of the Company. They were 1,500 tons larger than any earlier P&O ships. Mark Twain travelled in OCEANA in 1895 on a world lecture tour, and wrote "This is a noble big ship with spacious promenade decks, a luxury to travel in such". Sunk off Eastbourne in 1912 following a collision with the German barque PISAGUA. Gold bullion worth £700,000 was later salvaged from the wreck, at a depth of 90 feet.

Sister ships: VICTORIA, BRITANNIA, ARCADIA

CANTON (II)   Southern Chinese city

1889/1903.   Passenger/Cargo Liner, designed for cargo services between India and China.

Built by Caird & Co, Greenock. Although primarily built for cargo carrying in the China trade, she had accommodation for 26 passengers. Early in her career, towed SIAM (also P&O), with a broken shaft, from Aden to Bombay. 1900 served as a transport ship during the Chinese Boxer Rebellion. 1903 sold to Messageries Maritime, France and renamed BOSPHORE. 1922 sold to Italian shipbreakers.

Sister ships: BOMBAY (II), HONG KONG, SHANGHAI (II)

S/S Himalaya.

P and O

Port Said
15/3/04.

Arrived here last Evening, after smooth
passage. — This is a wicked place.
Best chin chin, Fred.

HIMALAYA (II)   Highest mountain range in the world, Northern India
1892/1916, 1919/1922.   Passenger Liner, employed UK/Australia, later India and Japan

Built by Caird & Co Ltd, Greenock, to Admiralty specifications under subsidy. The first P&O ship requisitioned in 1914, less than 24 hours after the outbreak of war. Converted in Hong Kong to an Armed Merchant Cruiser, and manned largely by her peacetime crew, under a Royal Navy Commander. Alterations included the fitting of eight 4.7" guns. In 1916 she was fitted with 6" guns, an aircraft deck and a seaplane. The Admiralty bought the ship in 1916, but the P&O contested their right to do this, and in 1919 HIMALAYA was resold to the Company. Broken up Bremen.
Sister ship: AUSTRALIA

R. M. S. CALÉDONIA

Peninsular Oriental Co

CALEDONIA   Poetic Latin name for Scotland

1894/1925.   Passenger Liner, Indian mail service

Built by Caird & Co Ltd, Greenock. She was the first P&O ship to use Tilbury Dock, in 1903. In 1916, whilst on a routine voyage, she struck two mines off Marseilles. All passengers and some crew were taken off within 15 minutes and a skeleton crew took her into Marseilles, where she was repaired for return to service. A year later she became a Troopship and carried in safety more than 104,000 troops until the end of the War. She returned to commercial service in 1920, but whilst in Bombay in 1925 her propeller shaft was found to be cracked, and she was sold locally for demolition.

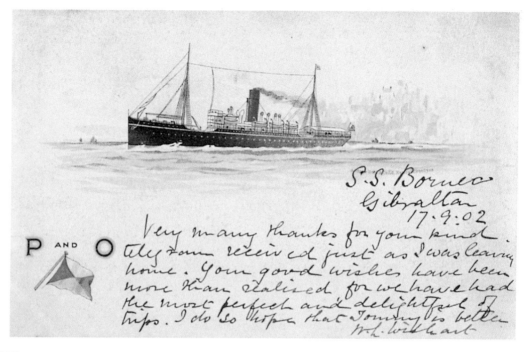

S.S. Borneo
Gibraltar
17.9.02

Very many thanks for your kind
telegram received just as I was leaving
home. Your good wishes have been
more than realised for we have had
the most perfect and delightful of
trips. I do so hope that Tommy is better
W.L. Wishart

BORNEO   Far Eastern island, third largest in the world
1895/1914.   Passenger Liner. Indian and Far East service
Built by Palmers' Shipbuilding & Iron Co, Jarrow. Mr Wishart, writing in 1902 (above), is clearly quite happy with the ship,
having had "the most perfect and delightful of trips".
Sister ships: SUMATRA, SUNDA, PALAWAN

R.M.S. CHINA
Péninsular Oriental Co
Night's view.
H. Grimaud, et cie, 54 Rue Marengd - Marseille

CHINA (II)　　　　　　　　　　　　　　　　　　　　　　　Huge Far Eastern country
1896/1928.　　Passenger Liner, Indian and Australian services

Built by Harland & Wolff Ltd, Belfast. 1898, homeward from Australia, she grounded on Perim Island in the Red Sea. There were no casualties, all passengers and crew being saved, together with the mail, baggage and the specie, although her cargo had to be condemned. Salvage took six months, but she eventually underwent major repairs by her builders and re-entered service. She spent the whole of the 1914/18 War as a Hospital Ship and was visited by King George V, who congratulated the Commander on the work his ship was doing. CHINA returned to her peacetime career in 1919. My Grandfather, en route for Bombay in the 1920s, commented in a letter that "My cabin is horrid but the pusser (sic) is giving me a 3 berth cabin to myself down below". He later said it was "Oh so hot", but he had played a lot of cricket and the swimming bath had "been up since Suez". CHINA was broken up in Osaka, the only one of the five sisters not to be destroyed by war or accident.

Sister ships: INDIA, EGYPT, ARABIA, PERSIA

INDIA (II)   Asian Sub Continent

1896/1915.   Passenger Liner, Indian and Australian services

Built by Caird & Co Ltd, Greenock. This postcard is a vignette of the type commonly used by the Company to illustrate all the vessels of a class, leaving the passenger to identify the particular ship concerned.

Sister ships: CHINA, EGYPT, ARABIA, PERSIA

India.

K.C.Lockwood.

INDIA (II) In 1915 she was hired by the Admiralty as an Armed Merchant Cruiser. Within five months, while serving with the 10th Cruiser Squadron, she was torpedoed and sunk by a German submarine off Norway. Those lost were 10 officers and 150 ratings.

P & O

S.S.EGYPT

EGYPT North-East African country

1897/1922.   Passenger Liner, Australian and Indian services

Built by Caird & Co Ltd, Greenock. From 1915 she served as a Hospital Ship in the Mediterranean, returning to P&O in 1921. Only a year later, her life was ended. Bound for Bombay, she was struck in thick fog off Ushant by the French steamer SEINE. 86 people died, but many more were saved by the presence of mind of the crew, who had only 20 minutes before the ship turned over and sank in 60 fathoms. She carried bullion worth over a million pounds, and persistent efforts were made to locate the wreck and recover the treasure. Eventually, in 1930, using new techniques and equipment, the Italian salvage vessel ARTIGLIO found the EGYPT. Over 90% of the bullion was recovered between 1932 and 1935.

Sister ships: INDIA, CHINA, ARABIA, PERSIA

s.s. "ARABIA."
7,933 tons.   11,000 h.p.

ARABIA   Large Middle-Eastern peninsula
1898/1916.   Passenger Liner, designed for Accelerated Indian and Australian mail contracts
Built by Caird & Co Ltd, Greenock. Sent from the "Mediterranean Sea", this card mentions "an awful passage as far as
Gibraltar, but its perfect today".
Sister ships: INDIA, CHINA, EGYPT, PERSIA

ARABIA

During the First World War, ARABIA maintained her normal voyaging to and from Australia and seemed to be a lucky ship, escaping three times from submarine attack. But in 1916 her luck ran out. Returning from Sydney, with passengers and general cargo, she was torpedoed and sunk South of Cape Matapan Greece. Eleven engine room crew died in the attack, but all the passengers, including children, were saved. One mother was separated from her baby in the rescue, to be reunited two desperately anxious days later in Malta. Afterwards, in reply to letters from the USA about the sinking, the Germans said the submarine commander thought the ladies' dresses were the uniforms of Chinese soldiers going to join the Allies in France.

P.&O. S.S. Isis.

ISIS   Egyptian Goddess
1898/1915 1920.   Passenger Liner; Shuttle Service Brindisi/Port Said

A delightful example of a ship's Christmas card. 1906 badly damaged after losing her propeller en route to Port Said. Temporarily repaired in Zante. War service from 1915 as HMS ISONZO, despatch ship. Laid up in Falmouth January 1920; in August sold to M.H. Bland & Co Ltd of Gibraltar, re-named GIBEL EL SARSAR. Laid up in Gibraltar in 1923. 1926 sold to Italian shipbreakers and broken up in Genoa.

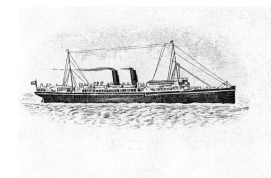

With Christmas Greetings
and Best Wishes
for the Coming Year
from

Jim with Love
+ kisses for the Boss

R.M.S. ASSAYE
Paquebot Poste Rapide Anglais à double hélices
de la Cie Péninsular Oriental
Télégraphie sans fil à bord

ASSAYE   Indian village, scene of a battle in 1803
1899/1928.   Passenger Liner/Troopship

Built by Caird & Co Ltd, Greenock. Designed for the Intermediate passenger service, ie between 1st Class and emigrant, but she actually spent most of her life as a Troopship. Some notes at the front of one set of her Articles of Engagement, which all officers and crew members were required to sign, state "Crew provide own uniform. No gambling or trading with the troops". In dense fog in 1904, she had a collision in the Solent off Hurst Castle with American Line ship NEW YORK. The latter lost her bowsprit and ASSAYE suffered a badly damaged starboard bow in the incident. 1914 hired by the Admiralty as a Troopship and later served as a Hospital Ship. 1928 broken up Stavanger, Norway.
Sister ships: SOBRAON, PLASSY

P. & O. S.S. "PERSIA" LEAVING MARSEILLES.
8,000 TONS, 11,000 HORSE-POWER.

PERSIA   Former name of Iran

1900/15.   Passenger Liner, UK/India service

Built by Caird & Co Ltd, Greenock. The ship's log for a voyage in August 1905 mentions that a certain John Seymour was "logged" (an entry made in the log) for stealing brandy, consequently charged in the police court at Bombay and sentenced to "4 months rigorous imprisonment in the House of Correction". I shouldn't think he helped himself to brandy again, after that—if indeed he ever had the chance. This card, bearing a Marseilles Paquebot stamp in 1911, says "At last we are on our way home and having a splendid trip not much like the Medea". The original painting is by W.L. Wyllie and is in the present P&O Art Collection.

Sister ships: INDIA, CHINA, EGYPT, ARABIA

P&O-R.M.S.PERSIA   8000 Tonns. 11000 Horsepower.

PERSIA

On a routine voyage homeward bound in 1915, she was torpedoed without warning off Crete. Her port boiler blew up, causing her to sink very quickly. She carried 501 people in total, 334 of whom died. Survivors were rescued by a trawler.

"PLASSY."

PLASSY   Bengal village, scene of a battle in 1757

1901/1924. Passenger Liner/Troopship. Intermediate passenger service, employed almost exclusively trooping and Hospital Ship

Built by Caird & Co Ltd, Greenock. The writer of this card in 1908 reports his safe arrival in Port Said and says he has not been sick (so far). This postcard also illustrates the two flags flown by a Troopship—the Houseflag at the main mast and the Blue Ensign, "defaced by a foul anchor" at the stern, symbolising her loyalty to her Company and to her service. PLASSY served as a Hospital Ship in the Great War and was visited by King George V, who, having inspected the ship thoroughly, remarked on how clean and efficient she was. Broken up Genoa.

Sister ships: ASSAYE, SOBRAON

Oakley, Photo. Copyright.   Troopship "Soudan"   Netley, Southampton.

SOUDAN (I)   North East African country
1901/25.   Passenger/Cargo Liner. Intermediate passenger service and trooping if required
Built by Caird & Co Ltd, Greenock. The writer of this card, probably a soldier writing to his wife, is cautious: ".....my first impression is favourable. I hope it will remain so. I could see you quite plainly as I went by. Don't I wish I was coming back instead of going ..... now try to keep cheerful and brave. It is awfully hard I know".
Sister ships: SICILIA, SYRIA, SOMALI, SARDINIA

F. G. O. Stuart. 1819   H. M. T. Somali

SOMALI (I)   People from the Horn of Africa
1901/23.   Passenger/Cargo Liner. Intermediate passenger service. Trooping if required
Built by Caird & Co Ltd, Greenock. 1923 laid up in the Fal River before being broken up in Denmark.
Sister ships: SICILIA, SOUDAN, SYRIA, SARDINIA   (Photo: A. S. Mallett Collection)

s.s. "SICILIA."
6,696 tons.   4,500 h.p.

P AND O

Feb. 18ᵗ 1912.

SICILIA
1901/26.   Passenger/Cargo Liner. Intermediate passenger service and trooping if required
Built Barclay, Curle & Co Ltd, Glasgow. In 1914 she became a Hospital Ship and was present at the Dardanelles. Broken up Osaka.
Sister ships: SOUDAN, SYRIA, SOMALI, SARDINIA   (Photo: A. S. Mallett Collection)

Egg & Spoon Race.

One of a series of tear-out postcards which P&O produced in a book, depicting scenes of passenger entertainment on board its vessels in the Edwardian era.

P. & O. S.S. "MOLDAVIA" AT BOMBAY.
(10,000 TONS, 14,000 HORSE-POWER.)

MOLDAVIA (I)   *European country, now part of Roumania*
1903/16—1917/18.   Passenger Liner designed for London/India or London/Australia mail service

Built at Greenock by Caird & Co Ltd. A card reproduced from a 1912 painting by Charles Dixon. 1915 MOLDAVIA was requisitioned by the Admiralty as an Armed Merchant Cruiser and compulsorily purchased, along with other vessels in a similar situation, in 1916. The Company held that they had no right to do this, and in 1917 the ships were sold back. In 1918 MOLDAVIA was torpedoed and sunk off Beachy Head in the English Channel. She was bringing troops from the USA, 56 of whom were killed in the explosion. Survivors were taken off by escorting destroyers.
Sister ships: MONGOLIA, MARMORA, MACEDONIA, MOOLTAN, MOREA, MALWA, MANTUA, MALOJA, MEDINA

MOLDAVIA (I)

The motto appearing on this card was changed to "Quis Nos Separabit"—"Who Shall Separate Us?"—in 1937 when the Company was granted its Coat of Arms. It may well also have had something to do with the fact that someone realised "Quis Separabit" was already the motto of the Irish Guards! "Quis Nos Separabit" is still the Company's motto. This trademark depicts, clockwise from top left: Britannia for the UK, an elephant for India, pagodas for the Far East and a camel for Egypt—no representation of Australia! The Coat of Arms, on the other hand, shows a British Lion, an Indian elephant, a Chinese dragon and an Australian kangaroo.

GREETINGS FROM INDIA.

By this card I'd like to say
How oft my thoughts are turned your way;
It also brings my wish most true,
That all is going well with you.

913.N.   COPYRIGHT.   BEAGLES POSTCARDS

A simply splendid card—just read the story in the pictures: a Royal Artillery soldier, who travels P&O to India (1903 M Class)—hands across the sea to his sweetheart, with roses for his love, ivy to enfold her and a nostalgic message..........oh my goodness!

MONGOLIA (II)   Central Asian country, now partly in China
1903/1917.   Passenger Liner designed for London/India or London/Australia mail service
Built by Caird & Co Ltd, Greenock. "Jack", who wrote this card, says "This is the sister ship to the Moldavia & nearly like
the Mooltan". 1904, MONGOLIA was intercepted by Russian warships in the Red Sea, possibly in the belief that she might
be Japanese, but allowed to continue once identified. 1916 the Admiralty hired her as an Armed Merchant Cruiser. The
following year, 50 miles South West of Bombay, outward bound, she struck a mine laid by the German raider WOLF. She
sank in 13 minutes, with the loss of 23 people. Most survivors met "desert island" conditions on the Indian coast, but the
Chief Officer's boat reached Bombay, and rescuers were sent.

Our Steamer, The "Marmora"

Aden, April 25.'06. Here we are & in good nick, Kind regards to you all and hope you are having cooler weather than exists here. R.H.B.

MARMORA Sea connecting the Black Sea and the Aegean
1903/16 1917/18.   Passenger Liner designed for London/India or London/Australia mail service
Built by Harland & Wolff, Belfast. Posted from Aden to a firm of solicitors in Dunedin, New Zealand, the writer of this card is "in good nick" and hopes the weather is cooler in Dunedin.
Sister ships: MOLDAVIA, MONGOLIA, MACEDONIA, MOOLTAN, MOREA, MALWA, MANTUA, MALOJA, MEDINA

S.S. Marmora

MARMORA

Served as AMC in the Great War and went through the same purchase/re-sale sequence as several of her sisters. In 1917, en route for Dakar from Cardiff, she was torpedoed and sunk, with the loss of 10 members of her crew.

Péninsulaire Orientale - Macédonia

MACEDONIA   Ancient European country, now partly Greece, partly Yugoslavia
1904/16 1917/31.   Passenger Liner, designed for London/India or London/Australia mail service

Built by Harland & Wolff, Belfast. I think the sender of this postcard, dated 17.4.09, must have been a member of the crew as he says on the back "Am sending this as it is a photo of my home for the last 4 months". There is also a remark that he "will indeed be glad to get home & clean out stove"—presumably a family joke. In 1914, whilst serving as an Armed Merchant Cruiser, MACEDONIA escorted the badly-damaged Cunarder CARMANIA to Gibraltar, after the action in which CARMANIA sank the CAP TRAFALGAR. Later the same year, in the South Atlantic, MACEDONIA was present at the Battle of the Falklands.

Sister ships: MOLDAVIA, MONGOLIA, MARMORA, MOOLTAN, MOREA, MALWA, MANTUA, MALOJA, MEDINA

15 PORT-SAÏD. — The P. O. Liners " Persia " and " Macedonia ". — L.

PERSIA and MACEDONIA

Before the First World War, alongside in Port Said: clearly PERSIA is waiting to join the Southbound convoy through the Suez Canal and MACEDONIA is homeward-bound having completed her transit of the Canal and about to enter the Mediterranean. "Bum boats" are attending both ships, acting as ferries to the shore, bringing mail and some supplies and almost certainly offering a huge variety of goods and souvenirs for sale to the passengers. One ploy, considered to make the vendors irresistible to passengers and crew, was to address the women by the name of some currently famous or notorious female, no doubt Lily Langtry in Edwardian days, Mrs Simpson in the late thirties and recently Princess Diana. By the time I was at sea, we were able to walk ashore from the foot of the gangway on floating pontoons, rather than using the bum-boats as ferries.

MOOLTAN (II)   British Indian garrison town, now in Pakistan
1905/17.   Passenger Liner designed for London/India or London/Australia mail service

Built by Caird & Co Ltd, Greenock. December 1905, on her maiden voyage, the ship's log records that Stewardess R.C. Barton, aged 29 from Dunedin, New Zealand, was landed at Port Said, with scarlet fever. A note on the ship's Articles against her name, where she should have signed off, says "Not allowed to sign". A story with no ending—poor girl, I wonder how she fared afterwards? Dated June 4 1910 this is a card from father to daughter. 1917 homeward bound from Australia and the Far East, with passengers and mails, MOOLTAN was torpedoed in the Mediterranean. Passengers and crew were saved by two Japanese destroyers.

Sister ships: MOLDAVIA, MONGOLIA, MARMORA, MACEDONIA, MOREA, MALWA, MANTUA, MALOJA, MEDINA

Peninsular & Oriental

Steam Navigation Company

Incorporated by Royal Charter

BOARD OF DIRECTORS

Sir THOMAS SUTHERLAND, G.C.M.G., LL.D., *Chairman.*	Major-General Sir OWEN TUDOR BURNE, G.C.I.E., K.C.S.I.
WILLIAM ADAMSON, Esq., C.M.G.	SAML. STEUART GLADSTONE, Esq.
The Right Hon. LORD BALFOUR OF BURLEIGH, K.T.	The Right Hon. THE EARL OF LEVEN AND MELVILLE, K.T.
HERBERT BROOKS, Esq.	WILLIAM GAIR RATHBONE, Esq.
The Rt. Hon. LORD BURGHCLERE.	PETER WILLIAMS, Esq.

Managing Director.—Sir THOMAS SUTHERLAND, G.C.M.G., LL.D.

General Managers.

F. R. KENDALL, Esq. | H. W. ULOTH, Esq. | H. H. JOSEPH, Esq.

Assistant Manager.   Secretary.
I. M. SHIELDS, Esq.   G. F. JOHNSON, Esq.

Manager, West-End Branch.—H. A. RITCHIE, Esq.

Auditors. { WILLIAM FRANCIS COURTHOPE, Esq.
          { FREDERICK AUGUSTUS WHITE, Esq.

Bankers.—WILLIAMS DEACON'S BANK, LIMITED.

Solicitors.—Messrs. FRESHFIELD.

LONDON OFFICES

HEAD OFFICE :	WEST END BRANCH :
122 Leadenhall Street, E.C.	Northumberland Avenue, W.C.

TELEGRAPHIC ADDRESSES

" Peninsular, London."	" Oriental, London."

TELEPHONE NUMBERS

PASSAGE & FREIGHT : 9467 Central.	
OTHER ENQUIRIES : 4205 Avenue.	5553 Gerrard.

3

Title page from the P&O Diary for 1906.

HANDS ACROSS THE SEA

H. M. Transport "DONGOLA"

DONGOLA (I)   Town on the river Nile, scene of a battle in 1896
1905/1926.   Passenger Liner designed for India China mail service and trooping when required
Built by Barclay, Curle & Co Ltd, Glasgow. "Hands across the sea" was a favourite sentimental greeting on postcards of the day. This one is dated 22.10.14 and sent from Liverpool by "Fred" to his mother: "Arrived here yesterday & disembarked today we are proceeding to Winchester... I am in the best of health. Grand voyage. Left Bombay 6th Sept". In 1923, whilst she was lying off Yokohama a tremendous earthquake occurred. The town was completely shattered and terrible fires ensued, with many casualties. The ship had to be hosed with water to stop her catching alight from burning oil in the harbour. DONGOLA took on board 600 injured and transferred them to Kobe. She was broken up in Barrow.
Sister ships: DELTA, DELHI, DEVANHA

S 2456   P. & O. S.N. CO'S S.S. "SALSETTE"

SALSETTE (II)   Island near Bombay in India, now connected to the city
1908/17.   Passenger Liner designed for express mail and passenger service Bombay/Aden

Built by Caird & Co Ltd, Greenock. She was an elegant vessel, the fastest ship in the P&O fleet and carried a large golden cockerel at her masthead to signify this fact. In July 1917, bound from London to Bombay, she was torpedoed and sunk by a German submarine South West of Portland Bill. Fifteen people died in the explosion and she sank within an hour, but all the survivors abandoned in the ship's own lifeboats and reached Weymouth. The Captain said the ship became dead and felt as though she was collapsing like a pack of cards.

P. & O. - S. N. COS - S.S. « MOREA »

MOREA   Peloponnese Peninsula, Greece

1908/1930.   Passenger Liner designed for London/India or London/Australia mail service

Built by Barclay Curle & Co, Glasgow. This postcard is dated 10 JA 12 and says "We have had a good journey so far—owing to a strike at Brindisi we have to go there for the mails, so have a chance of posting. We passed Stromboli last evening & thro' the Straits of Messina about 11.30 but too dark to see more than the lights. We sailed from Marseilles in glorious sunshine & have had a good passage except for rolling. We have a good cabin & are very comfortable. The Lascars were very smart today at their inspection". In September 1914, having left Sydney for London, her Lascar deck crew refused to remain on board beyond Bombay. So a Company of Royal Engineers who had embarked in Colombo, stepped in and crewed the ship home. 1930 broken up Kobe.

Sister ships: MOLDAVIA, MONGOLA, MARMORA, MACEDONIA, MOOLTAN, MALWA, MANTUA, MALOJA, MEDINA

P. & O. R.M.S. MALWA, 11,000 TONS, 15,000 HORSE POWER
India and China Mail and Passenger Service.

MALWA (II)   Central Indian state, now part of Madya Pradesh state
1908/1932.   Passenger Liner designed for London/India or London/Australia mail service
Built by Caird & Co Ltd, Greenock. This postcard is a reproduction of a painting by Frank H. Mason. Survived the First World War and almost certainly sank a submarine by collision in the Irish Sea. She was the last P&O ship to be hit by a torpedo in the war, but it was a glancing blow, and she survived this also. Broken up Osaka.
Sister ships: MOLDAVIA, MONGOLIA, MARMORA, MACEDONIA, MOOLTAN, MOREA, MANTUA, MALOJA, MEDINA

S.4838. my cabin ↑   P. & O. S. N. CO'S S. S. "MANTUA".

MANTUA (I)   Italian city and province
1909/35.   Passenger Liner designed for London/India or London/Australia mail service
Built by Caird & Co Ltd, Greenock. She went to Archangel during World War I, escorted by HMS DRAKE, to collect £8m in gold from the Russian Government, for safe keeping in London. The bullion was divided between DRAKE and MANTUA. Dated 1928, this postcard is from a mother to her sons: "We are at Southampton for the morning—I hear we damaged a propeller coming out of dock yesterday & a diver had to go down & look at it this morning & finds it's good enough to go on with, otherwise we might have had to wait 3 days to get it mended!" Broken up in Shanghai.
Sister ships: MOLDAVIA, MONGOLIA, MARMORA, MACEDONIA, MOOLTAN, MOREA, MALWA, MALOJA, MEDINA

S 4730   P. & O. BRANCH SERVICE, S.S. "COMMONWEALTH."

COMMONWEALTH   Named in celebration of Australia becoming a Federated Commonwealth in 1901
1910/23.   Passenger Liner employed Australian service via Cape of Good Hope Branch Line

Built in 1905 by Barclay, Curle & Co Ltd, Glasgow, for the Blue Anchor Line, whose funnel markings she shows in this
postcard. Following the tragic and unexplained total disappearance of the pride of the Blue Anchor fleet, WARATAH
(homeward bound off the Cape of Good Hope), P&O acquired Blue Anchor in 1910 for a very reasonable price. They
established their own Branch Line service via the Cape to Australia, with the five Blue Anchor Ships (the others were
WAKOOL, WILCANNIA, GEELONG and NARRUNG), all downgraded to Third Class only. P&O built five more
Third Class ships for the service. Blue Anchor funnel markings were retained until 1914. The writer of this card hopes to
send a better photo if he can get one. Broken up La Spezia 1923.

47

R.M.S. - "MALOJA"
Peninsular Oriental Co

MALOJA (I)   Swiss town and mountain

1911/16.   Passenger Liner designed for London/India or London/Australia mail service

Built by Harland & Wolff, Belfast. In 1916, on a normal outbound voyage, she struck a mine laid by a submarine off Dover pier. Although so close to land, there was great loss of life: 122 people died. To slow the ship, the engines had been put at full astern, but could not be stopped when the engine room flooded. Thus the boats could not be lowered and many were washed away as the ship charged astern, listing and flooding, to disappear within 20 minutes.

Sister ships: MOLDAVIA, MONGOLIA, MARMORA, MACEDONIA, MALWA, MANTUA, MEDINA

H.M.S. MEDINA LEAVING PORTSMOUTH FOR THE DURBAR

MEDINA   Isle of Wight river

1911/1917.   Passenger Liner designed for London/India or London/Australia mail service

Built by Caird & Co Ltd, Greenock. She was chosen to act as Royal Yacht and carry King George V and Queen Mary to the Delhi Durbar in India in November 1911 and did not enter Company service until the following year. During the War, she continued her commercial voyages, setting out from India on her final trip in April 1917. On board were the collected treasures of Lord Carmichael, retired Governor of Bengal. However, MEDINA was torpedoed and sunk by a submarine 3 miles off Start Point. Five crew members were killed. The ship's cargo of tin was salvaged in 1953, and most of the Carmichael collection was raised in 1987, although hopes of valuable treasure were largely disappointed. However, I was very interested to be able to acquire some encrusted items of Indian brass at the Sothebys sale the following year.

Sister ships: MOLDAVIA, MONGOLIA, MARMORA, MACEDONIA, MOOLTAN, MOREA, MALWA, MANTUA, MALOJA

S 9841   P. & O. BRANCH SERVICE S. S. "BALLARAT"

BALLARAT (I)   Australian town, Victoria
1911/1917.   Passenger Liner employed Australian service via Cape of Good Hope Branch line

Built by Caird & Co Ltd, Greenock. 1917, while serving as Ambulance Transport A70 with 1752 people on board, most of them Australian troops, she was torpedoed by a submarine South West of Wolf Rock. The troops' bravery and discipline were amazing—they abandoned ship in perfect order, halting instantly when a rescuing vessel could take no more. All were saved, but it might have been very different. The ship herself was not so lucky: taken into tow by a destroyer and HM Drifter MIDGE, BALLARAT sank in 44 fathoms off the Lizard the following day.
Sister ships: BELTANA, BENALLA, BORDA, BERRIMA

P. & O. BRANCH SERVICE S.S. BELTANA

BELTANA   South Australian town

1912/30.   Passenger Liner employed Australian service via Cape of Good Hope Branch Line

Built by Caird & Co Ltd, Greenock. The back of this card is worth quoting in full: "Dear Annie, We are on top deck & it is very nice the dining rooms is very large. nice reading rooms & Piana & all very nice class of People. no roughs only us trusting you are all well best love from me & Kit Mother (Aint you wild)". 1930 BELTANA bought by Japanese owners for use in the whaling trade. However, nothing came of this and she ended her days under her original name when she was broken up in Kobe in 1933.

Sister ships: BALLARAT, BENALLA, BORDA, BERRIMA

S 11354   P. & O. BRANCH SERVICE SS. "BENALLA"

BENALLA   Australian town, Victoria

1913/30.   Passenger Liner employed Australian service via Cape of Good Hope Branch Line

Built by Caird & Co Ltd, Greenock. In the First World War, her P&O Commander earned the DSC, for rescuing the British India vessel TORILLA from a submarine. BENALLA came upon the scene and attacked the submarine with gunfire until it disengaged from the encounter. BENALLA thereafter stood by the TORILLA until darkness. Soon after this she became a store carrier for the rest of the War. In 1921 she was beached in Pevensey Bay after a collision in thick fog off Eastbourne with the tanker PATELLA. Luckily her damage was not severe, and she was repaired in London. 1930 broken up Kobe.

Sister ships: BALLARAT, BELTANA, BORDA, BERRIMA

52

P. & O. S.S. "NELLORE" AT YOKOHAMA.
(7,000 TONS, 5,000 HORSE-POWER)

NELLORE   Town in Eastern India

1913/29.   Passenger/Cargo Liner designed for Intermediate London/Far Eastern service

Built by Caird & Co Ltd, Greenock. In 1916 in Malta, fire broke out on board, but she was beached, refloated, repaired and returned to service. She survived no less than 9 attacks by submarine during the 14/18 war, only to be sunk in the Indian Ocean in 1944, by a Japanese submarine, while under the ownership of the Eastern and Australian SS Co Ltd. She was en route from Bombay to Australian ports, carrying general cargo and Government stores. 35 crew, 5 gunners and 39 passengers died.

Sister ships: NANKIN, NOVARA, NAGOYA   (Photo: A. S. Mallett Collection)

S.14785.　　　　　　　　　　　　P & O. S. N. CO'S S. S. "KHIVA".

KHIVA (II)   Town in Uzbekhistan, on the old trade route to India
1914/31.   Passenger/Cargo Liner designed for Intermediate Indian service
Built by Cammell Laird, Birkenhead. Postmarked Dover 26 MAY 1923, this card remarks "There aren't a great many
people, quite half the passengers appear to be snotties.*" 1927 she was stranded near Steep Island 100 miles from Shanghai.
She was refloated, badly damaged. In 1931 KHIVA suffered a serious fire off Dairen, China and put into port, her main
deck gutted. Temporary repairs were effected, but it took her two months to return to London, only to be declared a
constructive total loss. P&O sold her to Japanese shipbreakers, which meant of course that she had to turn round and sail all
the way back to the Far East! * Naval slang for Midshipmen.
Sister ships: KHYBER, KARMALA, KALYAN, KASHGAR, KASHMIR

P. & O. S.S. "KARMALA"
(9,000 TONS, 7,040 HORSE-POWER)

KARMALA (I)   Western Indian town
1914/32.   Passenger/Cargo Liner designed for Intermediate Indian service
Built by Cammell Laird, Birkenhead. 1927 she served as a transport during troubles in China; she carried troops and armoured cars for the Shanghai defence force. Broken up Yokohama.
Sister ships: KHIVA, KHYBER, KALYAN, KASHGAR, KASHMIR

P. & O. S.S. "KAISAR-I-HIND."
(11,430 TONS, 16,000 HORSE-POWER.)

KAISAR-I-HIND (II)   Empress of India
1914/38.   Passenger Liner, designed for Bombay seasonal passenger service
Built by Caird & Co Ltd, Greenock. A very good looking and popular ship, her name meant "Empress of India", but my
Father told me she was always affectionately referred to as The Kaisar's Behind. He also said she had a plague of red ants at
one stage and was sent to the Arctic to try and freeze them to death, but I can find no Company record of this. At the Bod of
Gremista in Shetland, Arthur Anderson's home, there is a brass plaque of the P&O Rising Sun emblem. This was saved
from the ship at the end of her life by her 4th Officer, George Tweed, who later lost his life at sea during the War. His
brother presented it to the Museum. KAISAR-I-HIND was broken up in Blyth.

KAISAR-I-HIND (II) A fanciful depiction of the ship in a sea I am sure her passengers would never hope for. She is shown in the dazzle painted camouflage adopted in the First World War, and pioneered by the marine artist Norman Wilkinson.

Keepsake of Voyage

S.S. KALYAN
Peninsular Oriental Co

KALYAN   Indian town near Bombay

1915/31.   Passenger/Cargo Liner designed for Intermediate Indian service

Built by Cammell Laird, Birkenhead. The message on this card reads "Just a pc of the ship I am sailing on. It is a lovely Boat". She was a Hospital Ship during General Ironside's campaign against Bolsheviks. Based at Archangel, she was frozen in for an entire winter, becoming a temporary shore base. In the early part of war, lacking any armament, the ship mounted a pair of galley funnels to resemble guns. In 1927 there was a fire in the hold during transit of the Red Sea, outward bound for Yokohama. She put into Port Soudan and the fire was extinguished. Broken up in Osaka.

Sister ships: KHIVA, KHYBER, KARMALA, KASHGAR, KASHMIR

On board the SS "Kashmir"

KASHMIR

Northern mountain state divided between India and Pakistan

1915/32.   Passenger/Cargo Liner designed for Intermediate Indian service

Built by Cammell Laird, Birkenhead. An informal and cheerful group of officers, issued as a postcard. In 1918 the ship was involved in the loss of the Orient liner OTRANTO off the Isle of Islay. Both ships were proceeding in convoy, but KASHMIR's steering went wrong and she collided with OTRANTO, which drifted ashore on Islay. Rescue proved almost impossible, and 431 people were lost, many of them US servicemen en route for Europe. KASHMIR was seriously damaged and had to be towed to the Clyde for repair. She resumed her commercial voyages after the War. Broken up Osaka.
Sister ships: KHIVA, KHYBER, KARMALA, KALYAN, KASHGAR

P. & O. St. Nav. Co's and M. M. Co's Houses and Offices. Regimental Barracks
Steamer Point, Aden.

P&O Offices, Aden. This card shows the Company's offices in Aden, as they were between the Wars.

NALDERA North Indian hill village
1920/38. Passenger Liner designed for Australian service

Built by Caird & Co Ltd, Greenock, their last ship for P&O, before they were taken over by Harland & Wolff. She and her sister NARKUNDA were ordered in 1913, but work stopped at the outbreak of War. She was completed in 1918 as a Troopship, but never entered service. She commenced commercial voyages in 1920. On this French card she is mistakenly referred to as "R.N.S". Of course this should be R.M.S.—Royal Mail Ship, ie: a vessel under contract to carry His Majesty's Mails. Broken up Bo'ness. Sister ship: NARKUNDA

P. & O. S.S. NALDERA | THE BOAT DECK.
S.S. NARKUNDA
INDIA-CHINA-AUSTRALIA MAIL AND PASSENGER SERVICES.

NALDERA and NARKUNDA

A marvellous postcard. The atmosphere of power and security—almost of arrogance in the face of the world's oceans, is well conveyed. One can almost feel the throbbing of the deck under one's feet.

NALDERA

NALDERA was broken up comparatively early, at only 18 years of age. For one thing, although NARKUNDA was converted to burn oil, NALDERA remained a coal burner. Her final voyage was to have been a Government charter to Germany as a result of the Munich Agreement. The plan was to take the British Legion Volunteer Police to supervise the demarkation of the Czechoslovakian borders, but Hitler acted unilaterally, and the trip was cancelled. Had the Company kept her even another year, she could have given valuable service as a Troopship.

Port-Said. The Suez Canal.

NARKUNDA

North Indian hill village

1920/42.   Passenger Liner designed for Australian service

Built by Harland & Wolff, Belfast. The same early history as NALDERA. It was said during building, the two ships had been altered so many times at the Government's behest, that they had been everything but submarines. But once they were established on the Australian run, via Bombay, both vessels were extremely popular with passengers. Here the NARKUNDA is shown in the Suez Canal. NARKUNDA was a Troopship during the Second World War and in 1942, setting out for the UK after landing troops for the North African campaign, she was bombed and sunk by German aircraft off Bougie, Algeria. 31 crew members died in the attack.

Sister ship: NALDERA.

NARKUNDA

Happier days: in 1934 my mother travelled in the ship to her wedding in India. She recalls that married friends on board were asked to act as "chaperones", in spite of the fact that she was in her twenties. This card shows well the entertainment put on by the passengers themselves, before the huge changes in on-board entertainment which didn't really start till the 1960s.

NARKUNDA

First Saloon Divan: the narrow areas either side of the funnel casings always presented a problem. Here, a rather luxurious passage has been created between the foyer and the public room in the distance. The windows look out on the promenade deck and the design is still Edwardian.

S 15096.   P & O. BRANCH SERVICE T. S. S. "BARADINE". 13,300 TONS. ONE CLASS ONLY.

BARADINE (I)   Australian town and river, New South Wales
1921/36.   Passenger Liner employed Australian service via Cape of Good Hope Branch Line
Built by Harland & Wolff, Belfast. One of the second generation B Class ships built for the Branch Line service. They were
clumsy looking vessels which, with hindsight, would have been ideal as Troopships in the coming War, but in the thirties the
third class trade via the Cape declined and lost money even after a less frequent service was introduced. By mid 1936 all five
ships in the class had been withdrawn and the Branch Line service ended. Broken up Dalmuir.
Sister ships: BALLARAT, BALRANALD, BENDIGO, BARRABOOL

MOLDAVIA (II)   European country, now part of Roumania
1922/38.   Passenger Liner designed for London/India or London/Australia mail service
Built by Cammell Laird, Birkenhead. She originally had one funnel, but after trials a second dummy funnel was fitted, to improve her appearance. Broken up Newport, Monmouthshire.
Sister ship: MONGOLIA

MONGOLIA (III)   Central Asian country, now partly in China

1923/50.   Passenger Liner designed for London/India or London/Australia mail service

Built by Sir W.G. Armstrong Whitworth & Co Ltd, Walker-on-Tyne. This picture shows a Fancy Dress Party on board in November 1931, developed and printed on board by A.C. Yorke, Quartermaster. One of her cabins was reputed to be haunted, though there is no story as to why this should have been. In 1938 she joined the New Zealand Shipping Company and renamed RIMUTAKA. Re-sold in 1950 and had a series of owners and names: EUROPA, NASSAU, ACAPULCO. Finally demolished Osaka 1965.

Sister ship: MOLDAVIA.

R.M.S. MALOJA

MALOJA (II)   Swiss town and mountain

1923/1954   Passenger liner designed for the Australian mail service

Built by Harland & Wolff Ltd, Belfast. Both she and MOOLTAN were ordered in November 1918, but construction was delayed in the aftermath of the War. Both served as AMCs from 1939 to 1941 and then as Troopships. In peacetime, visits by the public to ocean liners in port were quite common for a long time (really, until the security scares of recent years) and this card sent to an address in the East End of London, on 8th August 1938, is from a little boy to his father. It says "Dear Dad, I saw the Baker & Butchers shop, Pantry, Engine Room, Stokehold, Bridge & Bridge deck, Cabins-de-Luxe of this ship. The baker gave me Swiss roll to eat. The chef was a great big fat man. Lots of love, Stan". Broken up Inverkeithing. Sister ship: MOOLTAN

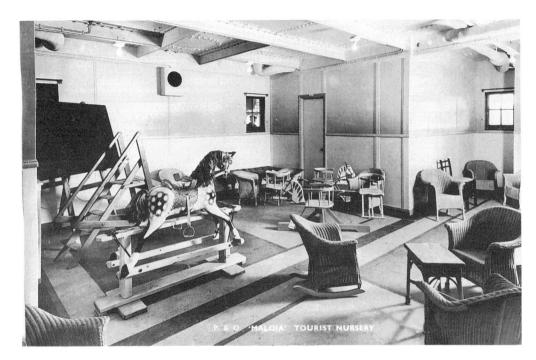

P. & O. 'MALOJA' TOURIST NURSERY

MALOJA

Small boys and girls travelling aboard after the War would have enjoyed the facilities of this cheerful Nursery, in the care of a Children's Hostess, while their parents were free to partake of the ship's other amenities, although nurseries were always closed whilst ships were in port.

MOOLTAN (III) British Indian garrison town, now in Pakistan
1923/54.   Passenger Liner designed for Australian mail service
Built by Harland & Wolff, Belfast. From 1939 to 1941 she served as an Armed Merchant Cruiser, but for the last part of the War, she was a Troopship. Her second (dummy) funnel, removed during this period, was replaced by a slightly shorter one after the War. Returning to Australia in 1953, she carried free of charge the Lord Mayor of Melbourne's regalia, used in the Coronation of Queen Elizabeth II. A well loved ship, on her last voyage, she was cheered away from every port including Bombay, where there was a routine change of Asian crew. The departing Goanese gave her a rousing send-off with their own top quality jazz band. Broken up Faslane.
Sister ship: MALOJA

P. & O. S.S. COMORIN, 15,000 TONS GROSS.
Australia Mail and Passenger Service.

COMORIN (I)   Cape Comorin, Southern tip of India
1925/1941.   Passenger Liner designed for the Australian service
Built by Barclay Curle, Glasgow. Suffered two serious fires, the second of which was to destroy her. The first in Colombo in 1930, caused massive cargo damage, although she reached London under her own steam for repair. 1939 requisitioned as an Armed Merchant Cruiser, after funnel removed, eight 6" and two 3" guns fitted. April 1941, in darkness, fire once again swept through the ship, whilst in the North Atlantic. In terrible conditions, 450 of her 470 complement were saved, many of them by the destroyer **HMS BROKE**, whose 1st Lieutenant, Peter Scott later painted a picture showing the nightmare operation in which **BROKE** came alongside the flaming vessel again and again in vicious seas, to allow **COMORIN**'s men to jump to safety. The blazing hulk was later sunk by the destroyer **HMS LINCOLN**.
Sister ships: **CATHAY, CHITRAL**

P. & O. S.S. "CATHAY" 15,000 TONS

CATHAY (II)   Poetic name for China
1925/1942.   Passenger Liner designed for the Australian service
Built by Barclay Curle, Glasgow. Requisitioned 1939 as an Armed Merchant Cruiser and converted in Bombay. Her after funnel was removed and armament fitted. Unscathed in this career, she was converted to a Troopship in Brooklyn in 1942, only to be bombed by German aircraft off Bougie, Algeria during the North African landings. A delayed action bomb exploded in the galley, causing an uncontrollable fire. The next day, this spread to the ammunition which exploded and blew off the stern. CATHAY rolled over and sank on her starboard side.
Sister ships: COMORIN, CHITRAL

P. & O. R.M.S. "CHITRAL" 15,000 TONS.
FAR EAST AND AUSTRALIA MAIL AND PASSENGER SERVICE.

CHITRAL (I)   Part of North West Frontier Province of British India, now Pakistan
1925/1953.   Passenger Liner designed for the Australian service
Built by Barclay Curle, Glasgow. Came safely through the War as an AMC, losing one funnel, as did her sisters. During her
final voyage a potentially tragic incident occurred, but there were no injuries. A cylinder cover burst and fractured the
cylinder, hurling metal debris. Her Chief Engineer and staff worked from Sunday morning until Monday afternoon, turning
her into a triple expansion vessel, enduring appalling conditions of heat and steam to effect this. They gradually worked up
speed till about 5 pm, when the engines were running smoothly and the ship doing about 14 knots. The passengers had
noticed something was wrong and presented the amazed and delighted Engineer Officers with a poem of appreciation,
signed by all the passengers. 1953 sold for demolition at Dalmuir.
Sister ships: CATHAY, COMORIN

CHITRAL (I)
The ship in her wartime colours, with only one funnel.

P. & O. S.S. RAZMAK, 10,600 TONS GROSS.
India Mail and Passenger Service.

RAZMAK   North West Frontier Province town, now in Pakistan

1925/30.   Passenger Liner designed for Aden Bombay shuttle service

Built by Harland & Wolff, Greenock. 1930 transferred to the Union SS Co of New Zealand and renamed MONOWAI.
Served as an Armed Merchant Cruiser until 1943 when she was converted in Liverpool to a Landing Ship (Infantry), in
which role she was present at the Normandy landings. She was returned to her owners in 1946 and reconditioned in Sydney,
to recommence her commercial career in 1949. She served until 1960 when she was broken up in Hong Kong.

RANPURA
                                                                    Small Indian princely state
1925/1944.   Passenger Liner, designed for London/India mail service
Built by Hawthorne Leslie & Co Ltd in Newcastle upon Tyne. A new class of vessel in P&O always introduced modern
improvements; the 'R' class contributed small refrigerated stores for fruit and fish, an electric lift and cabin radiators for 1st
Class passengers, and forced ventilation. The promenade deck ran right around the stern. Originally intended for the
London/Bombay mail service, the ship made a single round trip to Australia in 1929, after which she was put on the Far
Eastern service because Indian mails were by then being carried by Australian-service ships. In early 1936, RANPURA was
the centre of a small drama whilst carrying Chinese art back to Shanghai after an exhibition at Burlington House. She ran
aground when leaving Gibraltar; her passengers were transferred to other Company vessels, but she was quickly refloated
and, under protective escort of HMS VETERAN, returned her cargo safely to its Chinese home. In September 1937, in
Hong Kong, she survived a particularly terrifying typhoon.
78   Sister ships: RANCHI, RAWALPINDI, RAJPUTANA

RANPURA

An Admiralty photograph of HMS RANPURA, flying the White Ensign. In 1939 she was requisitioned as an AMC and converted in Calcutta. In common with many other ships, her after funnel was removed, but 11 feet of it had to be restored because of ventilation problems. These may subsequently have been solved, as the stump isn't visible in this photograph. RANPURA saw war service over a wide area, from the Eastern Mediterranean to the South Atlantic, convoy duty in the North Atlantic and patrol and escort in the Indian Ocean. She retained her P&O livery until a refit in Baltimore in February 1942, when she was painted Royal Naval grey, to remain so for the rest of her life. After the War, the Admiralty bought her outright and she served many years as a Naval depot and repair ship, being present in Port Said during the Suez Crisis of 1956. May 1961 sold and broken up in La Spezia. In a way, RANPURA still sails the oceans of the world, albeit on board ORIANA, where a large model of the ship in her P&O heyday dominates the Crow's Nest Bar.

(Photo: Royal Naval Museum, Portsmouth)

R.M.S. RANCHI

RANCHI   North East Indian town

1925/1953.   Passenger Liner, designed for London/India mail service

Built by Hawthorne Leslie on the Tyne. August 1939 she was requisitioned as an Armed Merchant Cruiser converted in Bombay, with the removal of her second funnel and the fitting of eight 6" and two 3" guns. After the fall of countries with North Sea and Atlantic ports, there was less requirement for AMCs, also more suitable naval vessels had been built and by the middle 40s, many surviving AMCs took on the new role of Troopship. RANCHI was converted for this work in Southampton in March 1943; the back of this card dated 1 Nov 1944, says "All these pleasure cruisers are doing noble war work". Later brought back ex-prisoners of war from camps in the Far East. She returned to commercial service in 1948. Broken up at Newport, Monmouthshire.

Sister ships: RANPURA, RAWALPINDI, RAJPUTANA

P. & O. C.Y. "RANCHI."

Dinner.

SOUPS.
Clear—Celestine   Thick—Argenteuil

FISH.
Fillets of Brill Orly

ENTRÉES.
Sweetbreads Florentine
Cauliflower Mornay

JOINT.
Roast Sirloin of Beef
Roast Quarter of Lamb

POULTRY.
Roast Duck   Salad

VEGETABLES.
Cabbage   Boiled and Château Potatoes

SWEETS.
Savarin of Fruits
Strawberry Cream Ices

SAVOURY.
Diablotins au Fromage

COLD BUFFET.
York Ham   Sheeps' Tongues   Galantine of Turkey

Dessert   :   Coffee

Sunday, May 2, 1926.

RANCHI

P.&O.C.Y.—the ship's designation on this 1926 luncheon menu—means "P&O Cruising Yacht", a term used by the Company before World War I and into the 1920's, but seems to have lapsed about then—this could even have been the last time it was used. It was probably only on cruise menus and not those for line voyages, but it does seem a bit incongruous for a 16,000 ton ship.

P. & O. 'RANCHI' FORWARD DINING SALOON

RANCHI

A post World War II view of the dining saloon—but the tables are still in rows rather than the more intimate tables for small groups of people characteristic of ships built after the War. At that stage in her career, RANCHI had been converted to a one class ship, to carry immigrants to Australia. Immigration to their country was encouraged by the Australian Government and the passenger was only required to contribute £10 sterling to the cost of the journey—hence the term "£10 Migrant". P&O carried not only British people to make a new life in Australia, but sometimes quite large numbers from other European countries. I remember STRATHMORE called for this purpose at Navarino Bay in Greece. Immigrants travelled in Tourist Class where there were two classes, but in one class vessels of course they had the run of the ship.

RAWALPINDI   Town in Pakistan
1925/1939.   Passenger Liner, designed for London/India mail service
Built by Harland & Wolff, Greenock. The first P&O ship both requisitioned in the Second World War and lost to enemy
action. 1939 Converted to an Armed Merchant Cruiser in the Royal Albert Dock, London. 23rd November in action with
the German Battlecruisers, GNEISENAU and SCHARNHORST South East of Iceland, until they sank her within 40
minutes with only a few survivors among her crew, one fifth of whom were P&O personnel. A brilliant painting by Norman
Wilkinson showing her vulnerable plating and upperworks ablaze, just before she sank.
Sister ships: RANPURA, RANCHI, RAJPUTANA

RAJPUTANA
Region of North West India

1925/1941.   Passenger Liner designed for London/India mail service

Built by Harland & Wolff, Greenock. In 1926 my Grandfather wrote: "This is a palace of a ship—wonderful public rooms and my cabin is splendid—a large cupboard, chest of drawers, proper washing stand, cupboard with little shelves for odds and ends". At the outbreak of war, she was requisitioned as an Armed Merchant Cruiser and converted at Esquimault, British Columbia. Her after funnel was removed and eight 6" and two 3" guns fitted. In April 1941 she was torpedoed and sunk South of Iceland, with the loss of 6 officers and 35 ratings.

Sister ships: RANPURA, RANCHI, RAWALPINDI

VICEROY OF INDIA   Head of British Government in India 1858-1947
1929/1942.   Passenger Liner designed for Bombay service, also cruising

Built by Alexander Stephen & Sons Ltd, Glasgow, she was a very special ship, and her interior was designed by Elsie Mackay, a daughter of the Chairman, Lord Inchcape. "The Viceroy" was involved in two major rescues following other ships' accidents, and picked up survivors from White Star liners DORIC off Portugal in 1935 and CERAMIC off Cape Town in 1940. Soon after, she was requisitioned as a Troopship and was converted on the Clyde. In November 1942, on her way home after taking troops to the North African landings, she came across a German submarine recharging its batteries on the surface off Oran, and was torpedoed. She sank with the loss of 2 Officers and 2 Fireman. The destroyer HMS BOADICEA rescued her survivors.

VICEROY OF INDIA
1929/1942.   Passenger Liner designed for Bombay service, also cruising
On the back of this card is written: "Full speed trial off Wemyss Bay $19\frac{3}{4}$ knots or over $22\frac{1}{2}$ m.p.h".

THE POMPEIAN SWIMMING BATH

VICEROY OF INDIA
The pride of the P&O, her public rooms were Baronial/Baroque and my Mother remembers particularly the red, green and gold of the Pompeiian swimming bath.

PORT OF LONDON.
NEW ENTRANCE, TILBURY DOCK.

Tilbury Dock. The "new" entrance to the Dock, built in 1929, showing P&O liners alongside in the distance.

P. & O. TURBINE-STEAMER "CARTHAGE." 15,000 TONS

CARTHAGE (II)   Ancient North African city, near Tunis
1931/61   Passenger Liner designed for London, Bombay, China service
Built by Alexander Stephen & Sons Ltd, Glasgow. September 1939 requisitioned as an Armed Merchant Cruiser and
converted in Calcutta, a lengthy, almost unbearably hot and uncomfortable experience for those of her crew who stood by
the ship. Her second funnel was removed and eight 6" and two 3" guns were fitted. 1943 her second conversion was to a
Troopship, in Norfolk Virginia. 1947 she was released to her owners. Broken up Sakai, Japan.
Sister ship: CORFU

P & O. 'CARTHAGE' 1st CLASS CABIN DE LUXE

CARTHAGE

Although small, CARTHAGE lost none of the available luxury of her larger sisters.

P. & O. 'CORFU'

CORFU   English name for Kerkira, Mediterranean island

1931/61.   Passenger Liner designed for London, Bombay, China service

Built by Alexander Stephen & Sons Ltd, Glasgow. 1939 requisitioned as an Armed Merchant Cruiser. Her after funnel was removed and eight 6" and two 12 pounder guns were fitted. 1944 converted for trooping duties at Mobile, Alabama. 1947 released to her owners and reconditioned in Glasgow by her builders. This card shows her after the War in her new white livery, with buff coloured funnel. CORFU and her sister CARTHAGE were extremely popular with passengers and ships' companies who preferred the intimate atmosphere of smaller ships. Broken up Japan.

Sister ship: CARTHAGE

STRATHNAVER (I)   Valley in Northern Scotland

1931/1962.   Passenger Liner employed London Australia service, also cruising

Built by Vickers Armstrong, Barrow in Furness, the first of the famous 'STRATHS'. In this photograph STRATHNAVER is shown with her original 3 funnels, on a pre-War cruising call at Venice. Requisitioned in 1940, STRATHNAVER served as a troop transport throughout the Second World War. In her book "Sister Sahibs", Marian Robertson, a VAD (Voluntary Aid Detachment) Nursing Sister, describes her journey to India in STRATHNAVER in 1944, no doubt typical of the hundreds undertaken by converted liners, when the discomforts and dangers were cheerfully endured in an atmosphere of friendship and fun unique to those times. The ship crossed the Atlantic twice en route to the Mediterranean from Glasgow, to keep clear of enemy planes and there were so many people on board that during the Suez Canal passage, all personnel were instructed to take up their Boat Stations positions whilst on deck, to keep the ship on an even keel.

Sister ship: STRATHAIRD

STRATHNAVER

Still in Government service, in October 1946 STRATHNAVER collided in Southampton with FLUOR, which sank at Berth 103. Returned to her owners in 1948. Recommenced commercial voyages in 1950, she and STRATHAIRD both having had their two dummy funnels removed. In June 1953 she was chartered by the Admiralty to carry official guests of the Government at the Coronation Review of the Fleet at Spithead. 1954 converted to one class and carried many "£10 emigrants" to Australia. Broken up Hong Kong in 1962.

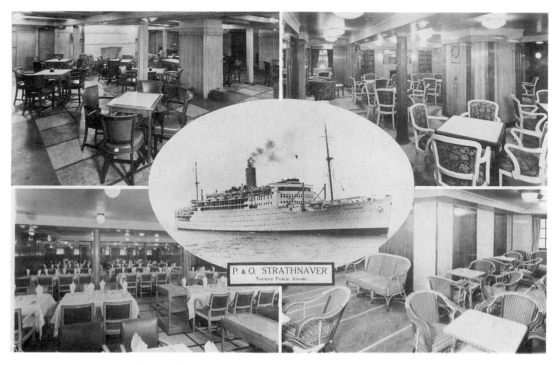

STRATHNAVER
A photocard popular in the 1950's, depicting the range of Tourist Class Public Rooms.

P&O R.M.S. "STRATHAIRD"   MAIDEN VOYAGE. 1932.

STRATHAIRD (I)   In the Southern part of the Scottish Isle of Skye

1932/61.   Passenger Liner employed London/Australia service, also cruising

Built by Vickers Armstrong, Barrow in Furness. This is a wonderful picture of her floodlit in Sydney on her maiden voyage in 1932. 1939, too large for an AMC, she was requisitioned as a Troopship and converted in Liverpool. She carried hundreds of servicemen safely until returned to her owners in 1946. After reconditioning, she recommenced service in 1947. In 1950 she was involved in the rescue of two Cocos Island boats. They set out to receive mail dropped overboard in a barrel from STRATHAIRD, a traditional way of delivery! The weather was so bad, that the plan was cancelled, but the boats had already put out. STRATHAIRD returned and under very difficult conditions, rescued the occupants of both boats and took them on to Fremantle. 1954 became one class. Broken up Hong Kong.

Sister ship: STRATHNAVER.

STRATHAIRD (I)

STRATHAIRD's swimming pool—still below decks; pools were not built in the open until STRATHMORE—but showing a clear Art Deco influence in design.

STRATHAIRD (I)

In Colombo harbour in 1961, almost at the end of her life. (Photo: Carola Ingall)

STRATHMORE (I)   Scottish valley, original home of HM The Queen Mother
1935/1963.   Passenger Liner employed London/Australia service, also cruising

Built by Vickers Armstrong, Barrow in Furness, best-loved of the STRATHs. 1940 requisitioned as a Troopship. On one trip Joyce Grenfell travelled in her to entertain the troops. Returned to her owners in 1948, to resume service in 1949. In 1956 she brought 11 Victoria Cross holders from Bombay for the parade in London, marking the 100th anniversary of the inception of the medal. 1961 converted to one class operation. 1963 sold to John S. Latsis, Greece. Renamed MARIANNA LATSI. 1966 renamed HENRIETTA LATSI. 1967 laid up at Eleusis Greece. Broken up La Spezia.

P. & O. 'STRATHMORE'

STRATHMORE (I)

An aerial view, which I sent home to my grandmother on my first working voyage in 1958. I made a pinhole (just visible) to mark my cabin—a lengthy screed on the back tells her I was having the time of my life! Because the ship was built before there were women in the Bureau (or Purser's Office), cabins were allocated to us on F Deck forward of the Dining Saloon. Having no air conditioning in the accommodation, it was sometimes hard to sleep at night when it was very hot, and the temptation was to have the scuttles open at all times; in rough weather the order would be circulated "Close scuttles"—once I forgot and was rewarded by the influx of what seemed like half the Red Sea drenching me and my bunk and sloshing about on the deck; luckily the coaming at the base of the door confined the flood to my cabin only, but I was pretty quick to slam closed the heavy porthole cover before the next wave came crashing in.

P. & O. 'STRATHMORE' · 1st CLASS READING & WRITING ROOM

STRATHMORE (I)

My favourite public room. We called it the Library. You can see a marvellous painting of HM The Queen Mother by Simon Elwes. As Duchess of York she launched the ship in 1934. The painting and other items were presented to her at the end of the ship's life. Films were shown in here, in the absence of a purpose-built Cinema—the big sofas were pushed against the windows on the starboard side (this view looks to port); we Junior Officers sat on the back of a sofa, our feet on the seat, and had a marvellous view of the screen!

CRUISING YACHT "VECTIS"

VECTIS (III)   Roman name for the Isle of Wight

1881/1912.   Iron Passenger Liner. Originally UK/Australia; latterly cruising

Built as ROME by Caird & Co Ltd, Greenock. In 1891 underwent modernisation, including the fitting of a new bow section and boilers, but before she could re-commence service fire destroyed much of her accommodation, which had to be rebuilt. In 1904 she was refitted as the Company's first official Cruise Liner, although earlier vessels had carried holiday passengers on line voyages. On cruises, VECTIS carried 160 passengers, First Class only. She made 10 to 12 cruises a year, a fortnight to a month in duration and calling at ports from Norway to the Adriatic, the Holy Land, Algiers and the Canary Islands. In 1912 P&O sold her to the French Government, whose intention was to convert her to a Hospital Ship, but this never happened and they sold her the following year to Italian shipbreakers.

Sister ship: CARTHAGE

P. & O. S.S. "SYRIA" AT PORT SAID.
7,000 TONS, 5,000 HORSE-POWER.

SYRIA (II)   Middle Eastern country
1901/24.   Passenger/Cargo Liner, designed for Intermediate
passenger service and trooping if required
Built by Alexander Stephen & Sons Ltd, Glasgow. 1924 broken
up La Spezia. Another wonderful Wyllie painting.
Sister ships: SICILIA, SOUDAN, SOMALI, SARDINIA

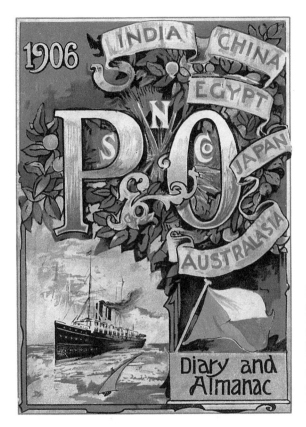

P&O Diary and Almanac: 1906. An enchanting little document, kept by Miss Nellie Robinson, of Southampton. Inside, there is a picture of MOOLTAN (1905) and throughout the year P&O anniversaries and record voyages are commemorated. There is a fleet list and the 1906 Pleasure Cruise Programme for S.Y. VECTIS, together with contract mail dates and time differences. Miss Robinson contributes addresses of her friends in the Navy, accounts of "very jolly" hockey matches and the fact that she received in total for Christmas the sum of £5 17s 6d.

P. & O. r.m.s. CANTON, 16,000 Tons Gross.
India and Far East Mail Service.

CANTON (III)   Southern Chinese city

1938/62.   Passenger Liner designed for London, Bombay, China service

Built by Alexander Stephen & Sons Ltd, Glasgow, the last liner to be built by them. My parents took me back to India on her maiden voyage, embarking at Marseilles, as so many did in those days, travelling by train across France, to avoid the stormy Bay of Biscay. My mother said CANTON was "like a little yacht". Initially serving as an Armed Merchant Cruiser in the Second World War, she was involved in a fight with several U-boats whilst escorting a convoy from Fremantle to London. During service on the Northern Patrol in January 1940, she ran aground on rocks off Barra Head, Isle of Lewis in the Hebrides. Damage was severe, but she managed to get off the rocks under her own power and reach the Clyde. In 1944 she was converted to a Troopship in Cape Town and released in 1947.

HIMALAYA
This evocative view featured on a 1960 P&O Calendar.

VICTORIA (II)   British monarch 1837/1901
1979/present.   Cruise Liner

CROWN PRINCESS
1990/present.   Cruise Liner

Built in Italy by Fincantieri, Monfalcone, having been laid down for Sitmar Cruises. She was designed by the Italian architect Renzo Piano, famed for the Pompidou Centre, Paris. She has an elegant "dolphin" bow, contrasting sharply with her "filter tip" funnel, a characteristic shared by her younger sister REGAL PRINCESS. Following the modern trend, rather than being "launched" on first taking to the water, the ship was named by the film star Sophia Loren in New York at a gala event, the climax to four days of celebration. Part of the Princess fleet.

ORIANA (II)

An impressive view of the liner as she sets off on her maiden cruise in April 1996.

STRATHMORE (I)

Stenographer—in this case, myself—before we were ranked Assistant Purser, presenting prizes at the Children's Fancy Dress in 1958. This was before the introduction of specialist entertainment staff, and we were often required to perform a dual role.

109

S.20337. P & O S. N. CO. LINER "STRATHEDEN" 23,722 TONS.

STRATHEDEN (I) Valley of the River Eden, Scotland

1937/64. Passenger Liner employed London/Australia service, also cruising

Built by Vickers Armstrong, Barrow in Furness. 1940 requisitioned as a Troopship. Released to her owners in 1947. 1950 chartered by Cunard for four Southampton/New York round trips. 1955 assisted the Greek trawler JASON, sinking in appalling weather off Cape Spartivento. Her first boat was overwhelmed with the loss of eight of her own crew, although four Greek seamen were subsequently saved. 1963, stood by CANBERRA as the two ships passed at night, when CANBERRA vanished, her lights extinguished due to an electrical fire. STRATHEDEN stood by to tow, but this proved unnecessary. 1964 sold to Latsis Lines and renamed HENRIETTA LATSI. 1966 swapped names with ex-STRATHMORE becoming MARIANNA LATSI. 1967 laid up at Eleusis. 1969 broken up at La Spezia.
Sister ship: STRATHALLAN

P. & O. 'STRATHEDEN' 1st. CLASS DANCE FLOOR

STRATHEDEN (I)

The "Dance Space", as we called it, was the background not only for dances, but for children's Fancy Dress parties, horse-racing nights, "Housie Housie" sessions and Church on Sundays. The Captain, or sometimes the Staff Captain, took the services, his Officers sitting in the front rows. In fine weather, the screens shown in the background were raised up to the deckhead, opening the area across the full beam of the ship.

STRATHALLAN

Scottish river valley

1938/1942.   Passenger Liner, built for the London/Australia service and cruising.

The last of the 'STRATH's, built by Vickers-Armstrongs Ltd at Barrow-in-Furness. Her peace-time career was very brief. Delivered without official trials on 10th March 1938 and shown arriving at Tilbury the next day. Requisitioned in 1940 as a troop transport and served until December 1942.
Sister ship: STRATHEDEN

(Photo: Courtesy of Museum in Docklands, PLA Collection)

STRATHALLAN

One of only two known (albeit rather indistinct) photographs of STRATHALLAN in her last moments, listing and on fire. She was carrying troops, nurses and military stores from Glasgow to Algiers. Almost at the end of her voyage, off the North African coast at 2.30 in the morning, she was struck by a torpedo fired by U.562. Four members of her engine room crew were killed. The destroyer HMS LAFOREY attempted to tow her into Oran, but after a huge explosion in her boiler room, STRATHALLAN was overwhelmed by fire and sank the following day. There were no further casualties, largely due to the coolness, discipline and gallantry of those on board and in the lifeboats.

CANTON (III)

A splendid view of the Boat Deck. Always a very popular ship with passengers and crew, she was broken up in Hong Kong in 1962.

SOCOTRA (II)   Indian Ocean island off the Horn of Africa
1943/1965.   General Cargo Liner, employed UK/India/Ceylon/Far East service

Built by Barclay, Curle & Co Ltd, Glasgow, P&O's only new vessel during World War II. In 1950 a cadet recalls that her "de-gaussing" equipment was still fitted. 1951, at Massawa, her steering gear was badly damaged after hitting a reef due to pilot error. Towed via the Suez Canal to Port Said, she proceeded from there under her own power, steering by an ingenious and complicated system of winches and wires. Despite her nickname of "SLOW-COTRA", her escort had difficulty keeping up – perhaps the imminent weddings of both the 2nd and 3rd Officers had something to do with this? 1952, the first of the Company's motorships to be converted to burn heavy oil. Seen here in Rotterdam drydock, on the left with SINGAPORE. Broken up in Hong Kong.

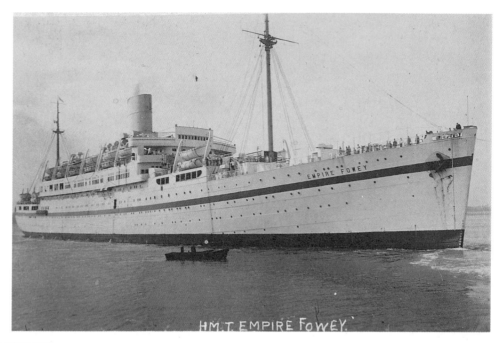

HM.T. EMPIRE FOWEY.

EMPIRE FOWEY   Troopship prefix "Empire"; Fowey a Cornish river
1946/1960.   Troopship, managed for HM Government

Built 1935 by Blohm & Voss, Hamburg; bought before completion by Norddeutscher Lloyd and named POTSDAM. During WWII, she ran the blockade from Hamburg to Lisbon and back, but thereafter remained in the Baltic until captured at Flensburg in 1945. Re-named EMPIRE JEWEL. 1946 re-named EMPIRE FOWEY under P&O management. Following lengthy conversions, including replacement of her experimental boilers, she emerged in 1950, the latest and best in Troopship design. A huge portrait of Hitler was replaced by a shield bearing the arms of Fowey in Cornwall. After their famous battle in Korea in 1951, she brought the Glorious Gloucesters home to Southampton. EMPIRE FOWEY was a happy ship, where relations between ship's Company and Army permanent staff were excellent and she was "adopted" by the Royal Engineers.

EMPIRE FOWEY

Withdrawn from service January 1960 and laid up in Portland until May, when she was sold as a pilgrim ship to the Pan Islamic Steamship Co of Karachi and renamed SAFINA-E-HUJJAJ, in which identity she is shown here. She sailed between Pakistan and Jeddah and from Pakistan to East Africa. Sold 1976 and broken up on Gadani Beach, Karachi. Beach demolition means the ship is literally run on to the shore and abandoned to her fate. It is hard to decide whether this is worse or better than a clinical dismemberment in dock; both are distressing for shiplovers.   (Photo: Carola Ingall)

DONGOLA (II)   Town on the river Nile, scene of a battle in 1896

1947/1961.   General Cargo Liner, employed Australia/India and later UK/India/Pakistan services.

1946 launched in Vancouver by West Coast Shipbuilders Ltd as Admiralty maintenance ship ORFORDNESS, but the War ended and she was sold to W.R. Carpenter (Canada) Ltd. Registered under Rabaul Steamship Ltd and completed as RABAUL. 1947 bought by P&O but managed by British India SN Co Ltd between 1949 and 1952. 1961 sold to Surrendra Overseas Ltd, India and renamed APJASHWINI. 1964 broken up in Bombay. Her somewhat spartan wartime design made life a trifle uncomfortable for her ship's Company, but she is nevertheless remembered with great affection by at least some of those who served in her.

P. & O. m.v. 'SOUDAN'

SOUDAN (III)   North East African country

1948/70.   General Cargo Liner employed Far Eastern service

Built Barclay, Curle & Co Ltd, Glasgow. In 1951 she carried 5 elephants from Southampton to Singapore for the Borneo Company, to overcome shortage of the animals since the War. On a subsequent voyage her cargo included 100 cattle from Singapore to Hong Kong; they walked on board, but had to be landed in slings on arrival. It was extremely hot but only three died. They were looked after by 2 Cadets who spent days throwing water over them to keep them cool and exercising them along the decks. Much cleaning was needed after their disembarkation! 1968 transferred British India, although still registered with P&O. Broken up Taiwan.

Sister ship: SOMALI

P. & O. m.v. 'CANNANORE'

CANNANORE   Indian West coast roadstead port

1949/72. Cargo Liner employed European and later Far Eastern services

Built by Barclay, Curle & Co Ltd, Glasgow. 1966 transferred British India though still registered P&O. A newly-appointed Chaplain to the Missions to Seamen sailed in the ship in 1970, on a fact-finding trip, to experience the seafaring life of his "parishioners". 1972 sold to Somali Republic and renamed SANTA ANA. Broken up same year in Taiwan.
Sister ship: COROMANDEL

HIMALAYA (III)   Highest mountain range in the world, Northern India
1949/74.   Passenger Liner employed UK Australia service, also cruising

Built by Vickers Armstrong, Barrow in Furness. Modern comforts included an evaporating plant to convert seawater, the first liner to be so equipped. 1950 HIMALAYA recommenced cruising, the Company's first since 1939. A "Thornycroft" funnel top to eliminate soot fall out, was fitted in 1953, followed by stabilisers and air conditioning in 1959. In 1956, in the Mediterranean outward bound, she suffered an explosion in a domestic refrigeration chamber causing the death of four crew members and injury to twelve others. 1963 converted to one class. 1970 she was the first to use the new passenger ship terminal in Kobe, marked by a Shinto religious ceremony. Always known as a smart and efficient ship, HIMALAYA was extremely popular with passengers and crew. She spent her last 5 months cruising from Sydney. Broken up Taiwan.

P. & O. HIMALAYA - 1st CLASS DINING SALOON

HIMALAYA (III)

A very clear picture of the table settings, which conveys so well the anticipation of an excellent meal, perfectly served. In the background can be seen the acid sand blasted gilt and silver mirror "Wild Duck" by Frederick Halford Coventry, a New Zealand artist.

P. & O. 'CHUSAN'

CHUSAN (III)   Chinese archipelago

1950/73.   Passenger Liner employed UK Far East, later UK Australia service

Built by Vickers Armstrong, Barrow in Furness, the largest P&O ship specifically designed for the Far East Service, and also the first large passenger ship to be fitted with stabilisers. This picture shows her before the Thornycroft funnel was fitted. In 1959 she was the first P&O Passenger Liner to circumnavigate the globe. In 1970, she was the last P&O liner to call at Bombay on a line voyage, and the same trip, the first to come alongside, rather than anchor in Colombo harbour, on her penultimate call there. She carried John Fairfax and Sylvia Cook to San Francisco in 1971, before their epic crossing of the Pacific by rowing boat. Towards the end of her career, she initiated cruising from Cape Town and she and CHITRAL took part in experimental cruises originating from European ports. CHUSAN was held in great affection all her life, a really successful ship. Broken up Taiwan.

123

CHUSAN (III) A dramatic view showing the bridge superstructure and Officers' accommodation. The writer says "We are now following your admirable example, & taking to the waters for our holiday".

GREETINGS

SINGAPORE (II)   Island at the tip of Malayan peninsula, now a republic
1951/72.   General Cargo Liner

Built by John Brown & Co Ltd, Clydebank. In 1964 renamed COMORIN II, and again in 1968, when her name became
PANDO COVE. With the idea of creating a corporate identity and a reputation for speed, efficiency and reliability, the
prefix PANDO was given to six other vessels in the Company's service: BALLARAT (PANDO CAPE), SURAT (PANDO
HEAD), BENDIGO (PANDO SOUND), and SUNDA (PANDO STRAIT), together with two transferred British India
ships: WOODARRA (PANDO GULF) and WAROONGA (PANDO POINT). This is a Company Christmas card, sent in
1959—an interesting comparison with the ISIS card.
Sister ships: SURAT, SHILLONG, SUNDA

P&O s.s. 'SUNDA'

SUNDA   Strait between Sumatra and Java

1952/72.   General Cargo Liner employed Far Eastern service

Built by John Brown & Co Ltd, Clydebank. In August 1953, after the British India ship CHINKOA suffered a serious breakdown, she towed the vessel home from Gibraltar to just off the Lizard, where she handed over to a tug. 1968 renamed PANDO STRAIT. Several P&O cargo ships, SUNDA included, had accommodation for up to 12 passengers. This was never exceeded, as it would have meant that a ship's doctor must be aboard—presumably medical attention was provided, in accordance with tradition, by the Captain and the Carpenter. Broken up Inverkeithing.

Sister ships: SURAT, SHILLONG, SINGAPORE

P & O 'PATONGA'

PATONGA

Australian town, New South Wales; also see below

1953/77.   Refrigerated Cargo Liner UK/Australia service

Built Alexander Stephen & Sons Ltd. Glasgow. Her name means "little wallaby"—her first commander had a wallaby wind-vane made in brass and fitted to the ship's foremast. 1975 renamed STRATHLAUDER. Broken up Karachi.

127

P. & O. 'BENDIGO'

BENDIGO (II)   Australian town, Victoria, founded on goldmining
1954/72.   General Cargo Liner UK Continent Australia service. Designed for wool trade
Built by Alexander Stephen & Sons Ltd, Glasgow. She carried the Olympic torch to Melbourne for the 1956 Olympics. 6
feet high, it was the same torch used in 1948 at Wembley. In 1968 renamed PANDO SOUND. 1972 sent Briton Ferry for
demolition, which did not begin for 16 months. In February 1974, during a storm, the hulk's moorings parted and it was
blown broadside across the River Neath, presenting a serious problem in its removal.
Sister ship: BALLARAT

P.&O. ARCADIA

ARCADIA (II)   Mountainous area in Greece, legendary Paradise
1954/79.   Passenger Liner employed on UK Australia service, also cruising

Built by John Brown & Co Ltd, Clydebank. A popular and reliable ship, whose career lasted 25 years. 1959 refit in Belfast
included full air conditioning. Here, I was also tempted to sleep with fresh air—but for the opposite reason from
STRATHMORE: it could be so chilly at night that many of us opened our portholes just to keep warm, not realising we
were messing up the air conditioning system—until we were told in no uncertain terms—and the scuttles were fixed in the
closed position! In November 1959, I was among ARCADIA's ship's Company when she became the first cruise liner to visit
Picton in the South Island of New Zealand, a totally unsophisticated place amid glorious fiord scenery. 1970 ARCADIA
converted to one-class cruising and in 1976 permanently based in Sydney. Broken up Taiwan.
Sister ship: IBERIA

P & O ARCADIA 1st CLASS OBSERVATION LOUNGE

ARCADIA (II)

The Observation Lounge. This was a magnificent room, under the Bridge and spanning almost the whole breadth of the ship. The view forward through curved windows could be spectacular, whether looking out over the bows in a heavy sea or, perhaps contemplating the Panama Canal, a drink in your hand. IBERIA had the same facility, but ARCADIA's room was distinguished by the presence of two globes, one of the earth, and the other of the sky.

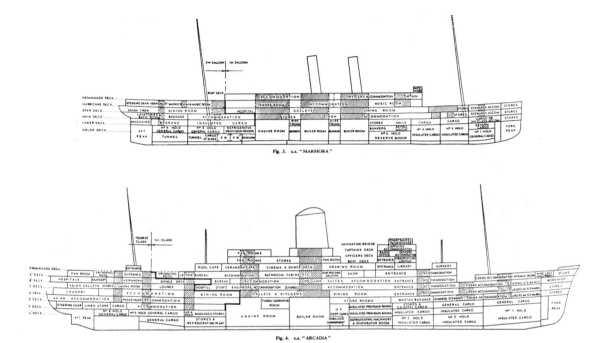

Fig. 3. s.s. "MARMORA"

Fig. 4. s.s. "ARCADIA"

MARMORA (1903) and ARCADIA (1954)

An interesting comparison of the fore and aft layout of the two vessels. Although ARCADIA is much bigger (29,734 tons as opposed to 10,509) the basic arrangements are very similar.

IBERIA (II)   Spanish/Portuguese Peninsula
1954/1972.   Passenger Liner employed on UK Australia service, also cruising
Built by Harland & Wolff, Belfast. 1956 she sustained extensive damage when in collision off Colombo with tanker
STANVAC PRETORIA. Repairs were carried out in Sydney. 1960 full air conditioning was installed during a refit in
Southampton. Soon after, she undertook a 5-month round world voyage, crossing the Pacific 3 times. During the trip, one of
the Assistant Pursers completely "lost" his 21st birthday crossing the International Date Line. Sadly, although IBERIA was a
happy ship, she suffered from persistent mechanical problems, and she was the first of the post-war passenger ships to be
withdrawn.
Sister ship: ARCADIA

P & O IBERIA 1ST CLASS SPORTS DECK

IBERIA (II)

Many P&O ships were "adopted" by schools through The British Ship Adoption Society, but IBERIA's connection with the Florence Treloar School, Alton, Hampshire, was rather special: This was a school for handicapped girls, in aid of which donations were collected on board. On at least one occasion, girls from the school spent a most enjoyable day on board IBERIA. Broken up Taiwan.

CATHAY (III)   Poetic name for China
1961/76.   Passenger Liner
Built 1957 by SA Cockerill-Ougree, of Hoboken, Belgium, as BAUDOINVILLE for Compagnie Maritime Belge (Lloyd
Royale) SA. 1961 bought by the Company with her sister JADOTVILLE for their Far Eastern Service, to replace
CARTHAGE and CORFU. The 1967 closure of the Suez Canal seriously disrupted their services and it was decided to
transfer them to the Eastern and Australian SS Co Ltd, a subsidiary of P&O, CATHAY in 1969 and CHITRAL in 1970.
1976 CATHAY sold to Nan Yang Shipping Co, renamed KENGHSING. Later named SHANGHAI and registered to the
China Ocean Shipping Co. In service until 1996, when she was reported to have been sold for breaking up in China. Here
she is shown as the SHANGHAI in Hong Kong harbour.
Sister ship: CHITRAL   (Photo: Paul Morgan: Chantry Classics)

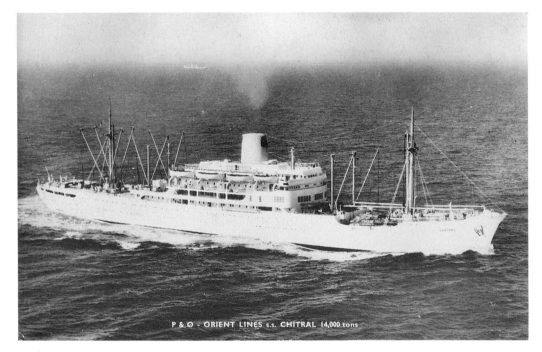

P & O - ORIENT LINES s.s. CHITRAL 14,000 tons

CHITRAL (II)   North West Frontier Province of British India, now Pakistan
1961/70 1971/75.   Passenger Liner UK Far Eastern service

Built 1955 by Chantier et Ateliers, St Nazaire, for Compagnie Maritime Belge (Lloyd Royale) SA, as JADOTVILLE. 1970 she made the final P&O passenger voyage from UK to the Far East and the same year was the last P&O Passenger Liner to use the Royal Docks in London. She then joined the Eastern & Australian SS Co Ltd, to be based in Sydney. Both she and her sister needed to function profitably in the carriage of cargo as well as passengers, and the development of container traffic began to affect them badly in the former capacity. Thus, their Australia-based careers were short-lived and CHITRAL was the first to be sold in 1975, when she was broken up in Taiwan.
Sister ship: CATHAY

CANBERRA　　　　　　　　　　　　　Australian Capital City, Aboriginal: "Meeting Place"

1961/In service until 1997.　Passenger Liner and Cruise ship

Built by Harland & Wolff, Belfast, a ship of revolutionary design. From her maiden voyage, she was in the news: she has been rescuer and rescued, announced for sale and then reprieved, often the centre of controversy, but always held in great affection by her changing ship's Company down the years, as well as faithful passengers who travelled in the ship time after time. This postcard was sold on board during the Maiden Voyage. Originally, she undertook liner voyages to the West Coast of Canada and the USA, via the Suez Canal, Australia, New Zealand and Honolulu, returning by the same route, but after 1973 she was exclusively a Cruise ship. She has never been converted from steam. After 36 years in service, and still extremely popular, CANBERRA is about to "sail into the sunset", largely because of new SOLAS regulations. The cost of refit to meet the requirements is considered unjustified and she is to be withdrawn in September 1997, her future at present a question mark. CANBERRA will be missed—a much loved and unique vessel.

CANBERRA

In 1963, outward bound, she caught fire off Malta after an electrical explosion and was crippled for some hours. STRATHEDEN stood by to take off passengers, and if necessary provide a tow, but CANBERRA managed eventually to re-start one engine and make it to Malta under her own steam. In later years, her role was reversed when she came upon a family adrift in the Pacific, after their boat had been sunk by a whale, and took them on board. In 1970 she carried to Port Everglades, Florida one of Captain Cook's salvaged cast iron cannons, thrown overboard when the ENDEAVOUR went aground on the Great Barrier Reef in 1770. One of six recovered, the gun was donated to the Philadelphia Academy of Natural Sciences in recognition of their work in locating ENDEAVOUR's armament. (Photo: Carola Ingall)

137

CANBERRA

During the conflict with Argentina in 1982, she was requisitioned as a Troopship. As well as troops carried from Britain, those from QUEEN ELIZABETH 2 were transferred to CANBERRA off South Georgia. CANBERRA sailed twice into San Carlos Water where, although she presented an almost "sitting duck" target, all her troops were disembarked for the landings and she emerged unscathed. Later, she repatriated Argentinian prisoners of war, before returning to the UK with British troops, to an ecstatic welcome in Southampton. (Photo: Prescott-Pickup & Co Ltd)

MALOJA (III)   Swiss town and mountain
1971/1976.   Tanker

Built in 1959 by Smith's Dock Co Ltd at Middlesbrough for Charter Shipping Co Ltd, a subsidiary Company set up, for tax advantage, in Bermuda. Initially managed by P&O for this Company, with MANTUA (II) and MALWA (III). The 15 ships in the original tanker programme were at first managed and operated by individual companies in the Group, but in 1962 Trident Tankers was formed to take over operation and management of all Group tankers, eventually the largest British tanker fleet outside the ownership of oil companies. 1964 management of MALOJA was transferred to Trident and in 1971, after total reorganisation of the P&O Group, to P&O Bulk Shipping Division. 1976 the ship was sold for demolition and broken up in Taiwan. In this photograph, taken by Captain "Dickie" Firth, MALOJA is shown "dressed overall", P&O's rising sun badge clearly visible on the bow.   (Photo: Captain R.N. Firth)

STRATHCARRON   Scottish valley, containing Carron Water SW Ross & Cromarty

1971/1979.   General Cargo Liner employed on Japan/Gulf service

Built 1969 by Swan Hunter Shipbuilders Ltd, Wallsend for BISN Co Ltd as AMRA. 1973 registered P&O but not renamed STRATHCARRON until 1976. 1978 registered Strick Line; 1979 sold Hyundai International and renamed HALLA PRIDE. 1979 suffered serious damage on going aground in Busan, South Korea, loaded with steel products. Repaired Ulsan; 1980 transferred Halla Maritime Corporation, South Korea; 1984 sold to Hyundai Merchant Marine Co Ltd, South Korea and renamed HYUNDAI No 33. 1985 sold and demolished Ulsan, South Korea.

STRATHCONON (I)   The valley of Conon Water, SW Ross and Cromarty, Scotland
1967/1979.   General Cargo Liner employed on UK/Far Eastern service
Built for the Company by Mitsui Zosen, Tamano, Japan: this photograph shows her under construction. 1977 transferred to
Strick Line; 1979 sold United Thai Shipping Corporation Ltd, Thailand and renamed CHUANGCHOM. 1980 her career
seemed to have come to a sudden end following her stranding in the Red Sea on Sha'b Abu Nuhas reefs. Her cargo was
saved and she was refloated but declared a constructive total loss. However, her new Greek owners A. Halcoussis & Co, had
her repaired in Piraeus, renamed her TZELEPI and registered her under Zannis Compania Naviera S.A, managed by
Halcoussis. 1984 demolished Shanghai.

SPIRIT OF LONDON / SUN PRINCESS (I) Princess names follow on from first vessel chartered by Princess Cruises' original owners PRINCESS PATRICIA
1972/1988.   Cruise Liner.
Built by Cantieri Navali Del Tirreno E Riuniti SPA, Genoa, ordered by Klosters R/A, Norway. Bought by P&O on the stocks and named SPIRIT OF LONDON to reflect the London theme of her interior design, but unfortunately many people nicknamed her the Gin Palace. 1974 renamed SUN PRINCESS. 1986 joined Princess Cruises fleet. In 1983 she saved the pilot of a small aircraft which ditched off the Alaskan coast: the ship first illuminated the ditching area, then picked up the pilot who spent the night in the ship's hospital, none the worse for his experience. Commended by US Coastguard. 1988 sold to Premier Cruise Lines, USA and renamed STARSHIP MAJESTIC; in this identity she suffered a serious fire in 1991, fortunately with no casualties. 1994 sold to CTC Cruise Line and renamed SOUTHERN CROSS.

SUN PRINCESS (I)
Cruising with ISLAND PRINCESS in background.

JEDFOREST 154,900 dw tonnes
Oil/bulk/ore carrier
P&O Bulk Shipping Division

Scottish Fox Hunt

JEDFOREST

1972/1987.   Ore/Bulk/Oil Carrier, Chartered to Associated Bulk Carriers Ltd.

Built for the Company by Eriksbergs M/VA/B (Lindholmen Division), Gothenberg, Sweden. Constructed in 2 parts: the stern and 4 holds by Eriksbergs and the bow/midship section including 6 holds by Lisnave Estaleiros Navais de Lisboa S.a.r.l., Lisbon, Portugal. The stern was towed to Gothenberg and the ship joined together there. 1977 transferred to Orient SN Co Ltd. 1986 registered Hong Kong. 1987 sold to Tradeshores Line Ltd, Cyprus and renamed LADY SKY. Whilst on the Kharg Island "shuttle service" she was attacked and set on fire by Iraqi aircraft, but repaired and returned to service.

ISLAND PRINCESS
1974/present.   Cruise Liner
1971 built by Rheinstahl Nordseewerke of Emden for Norwegian Cruiseships A/S of Oslo as ISLAND VENTURE. 1972 renamed ISLAND PRINCESS. 1974 purchased by P&O. 1989 voted America's favourite Cruise ship. In the present fleet. The ship has been well known for many years for voluntary weather reporting, and has received a record number of awards from the Government of Canada. Seen in Glacier Bay September 1986.
Sister ship: PACIFIC PRINCESS

(Photo: Captain Philip Jackson)

PACIFIC PRINCESS
1975/present.   Cruise Liner
Built 1971 by Rheinstahl Nordseewerke of Emden for Norwegian Cruiseships A/S of Oslo as SEA VENTURE. P&O bought her in 1975 and renamed her PACIFIC PRINCESS. She is the star of the TV series The Love Boat and is a member of the Princess fleet, based in California.
Sister ship: ISLAND PRINCESS   (Photo: Matt Southard)

PACIFIC PRINCESS

A spectacular night shot at Greenwich in 1987, when HM Queen Elizabeth II attended a gala dinner on board marking the 150th anniversary of the founding of P&O.

SEA PRINCESS (I) / **VICTORIA** (II) British monarch 1837/1901

1979/present.   Cruise Liner

Built 1965 by John Brown & Co, Clydebank for Swedish America Line, named KUNGSHOLM. 1975 sold to Flagship Cruises. 1978 purchased by Finance for Shipping Ltd, leased P&O Cruises. Refitted Vegesack, W.Germany, including removal of the forward funnel and increase in passenger accommodation. 1979 renamed SEA PRINCESS and delivered to P&O. She still has her original artwork, depicting scenes of Swedish history. In 1992, she rescued 371 passengers from the Cruise Liner OCEAN PEARL when the latter caught fire off Sumatra, in a mammoth operation involving high qualities of skill from all departments. In April 1995 she was re-named VICTORIA (II) to distinguish her from the Princess fleet and as a name more in keeping with CANBERRA and the new ORIANA.

SEA PRINCESS
Passengers enjoying the pool.

SEA PRINCESS
Alongside at Southampton preparing for another cruise.
(Photo: Carola Ingail)

ROYAL PRINCESS

1984/present.   Cruise Liner

Built for P&O by Oy Wartsila, Ab, Helsinki. Named by HRH The Princess of Wales at Southampton. The ship was the first P&O of the "new generation", featuring a short forecastle, very high passenger decks and a squared stern, but nevertheless an elegant vessel. She has been seen in ports around the world, where she is always a welcome visitor—a popular Cruise ship.   (Photo: Carola Ingall)

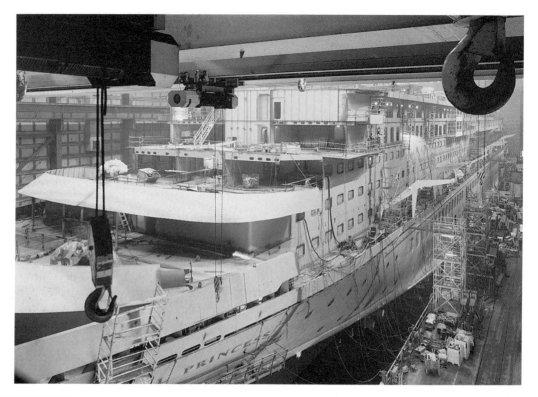

ROYAL PRINCESS
Work in progress at the Wartsila Yard, Helsinki.

FAIR PRINCESS

1988/present.   Cruise Liner

Built 1955 by John Brown & Co Ltd, Clydebank, as CARINTHIA for the Cunard Line. 1968 sold to Fairland Shipping Corporation, Monrovia and renamed FAIRLAND. Laid up in Southampton until 1970 and sent to Trieste for reconditioning. In 1971 transferred to the Fairsea Shipping Corporation of Liberia, and renamed FAIRSEA, before another transfer to Sitmar Cruises in 1980. In 1988 P&O bought the ship and renamed her FAIR PRINCESS and she joined the Princess fleet. Her planned sale in 1995 to Regency Cruises fell through and she was laid up on the west coast of America until early 1997; when, after refit, she replaced FAIRSTAR based in Australia.

Sister ships: SAXONIA, IVERNIA and SYLVANIA   (Photo: Clive Harvey)

DAWN PRINCESS (I)
1988/93.   Cruise Liner

Built 1956 by John Brown & Co Ltd, Clydebank, as SYLVANIA for the Cunard Line. 1968 sold to Fairwind Shipping Corporation, Monrovia and renamed FAIRWIND. Her ownership history runs parallel to that of her sister FAIRLAND but in 1980 her name was slightly altered to SITMAR FAIRWIND. She served with the Princess fleet as DAWN PRINCESS until she was sold in 1993 to Happy Days Shipping Ltd and renamed ALBATROS, making the headlines in 1997 when she went aground off the Isles of Scilly.
Sister ships: SAXONIA, CARINTHIA and IVERNIA

SKY PRINCESS

1988/present.   Cruise Liner

Built 1982 for Sitmar Cruises by Chantiers du Nord et de la Mediterranee, La Seyne, France, named FAIRSKY. 1988 became part of the Princess fleet with the acquisition of Sitmar by P&O. In 1990 re-registered under the Red Ensign. She and CANBERRA are the only two remaining steamships in the P&O fleets.

FAIRSTAR Sitmar prefix "Fair" retained 1988/1997. Cruise Liner

Built by Fairfield Shipbuilding & Engineering Co Ltd, Govan in 1956 as OXFORDSHIRE, a Troopship, the cost of which was shared between the Government and the Bibby Line. At the end of 1962 trooping requirements ceased. 1963 chartered to the Fairline Shipping Corporation, who bought the ship in 1964, renamed FAIRSTAR, to be operated between Southampton and Brisbane. In 1973 commenced cruising from Sydney, Australia. 1988 acquired by P&O. Her career was threatened in 1991 when she experienced a total breakdown on her way home to Sydney, carrying passengers, after a refit in Singapore. Her passengers had to be landed and the ship returned to Singapore for repairs. The old trooper found herself a place in Australian hearts and proved extremely popular, but was withdrawn in January 1997.

(Photo: Roberts & Wrate Ltd, Portsmouth)

STAR PRINCESS / ARCADIA (III)

1989/present.   Cruise Liner

Built by Chantiers de l'Atlantique, St Nazaire, France, the first of the Sitmar newbuildings that were taken over with the existing fleet. Laid down as FAIRMAJESTY. Her builders received Lloyds Register of Shipping's highest award, their Quality Assurance Certificate, only the third European shipyard to achieve this. STAR PRINCESS was their first ship to be so classified. Her naming was a star occasion in Port Everglades, Florida, her home port. The ship was met by a flotilla of small vessels, and festivities lasted a week. Film star Audrey Hepburn did the honours. The vessel has a unique collection of original contemporary art works, worth over a million dollars. On the withdrawal from service of CANBERRA in 1997, she is to be transferred to the UK-based fleet and renamed ARCADIA.

STAR PRINCESS / ARCADIA (III)
Passengers enjoying the two swimming pools during a cruise.

Featuring some of the most spacious passenger cabins in the industry, Princess Cruises' Crown Princess also has more veranda staterooms – a total of 184 – than any ship its size. Clockwise from top left:

- Suite with Private Veranda (575 square feet)
- Mini Suite with Private Veranda (382 square feet)
- Outside Double with Private Veranda (210 square feet)

Standard inside and outside cabins (not pictured) measure an impressive 195 square feet.

REGAL PRINCESS

1991.   Cruise Liner

Built by Fincantieri, Monfalcone, Italy and designed by the same architect as her sister CROWN PRINCESS, Renzo Piano. She was laid down for Sitmar Cruises. Mrs Margaret Thatcher, former United Kingdom Prime Minister, named the ship at a ceremony in New York in August 1991. Mrs Thatcher joined the ship at Pier 88 the previous day, for a gala evening, before sailing down to Pier 8 past the Statue of Liberty, accompanied by a firework display, for the naming event. The ship has a million dollar art collection of unsurpassed quality on board, and her public rooms include a Bengal Bar, reflecting nostalgia for the days of the British Raj in India.

GOLDEN PRINCESS
1994/1996.   Cruise Liner
Built for Det Nordenfjeldske D/S (Royal Viking Line) by Wartsila in Helsinki in 1972 as ROYAL VIKING SKY. 1982 lengthened by 91 feet in Bremerhaven, by insertion of a pre-fabricated midships section. 1984 bought by Norwegian Caribbean Lines A/B, 1987 passed to Kloster Cruise Ltd and renamed SUNWARD; 1992 sold to Birka Line A/B and named BIRKA QUEEN. Chartered P&O 1993 to replace DAWN PRINCESS, her charter came to an end in December 1996. Had Finnish officers.

ORIANA (II)   Poetic name associated with Queen Elizabeth I
1995.   Cruise Liner

Built by Meyer Werft at Papenburg, Germany. Her first journey was a nail-biting progress down the River Ems with only a few inches to spare below her keel. At 24 knots, ORIANA is the fastest Cruise ship built in 25 years. Joined CANBERRA and VICTORIA, with a world-wide cruising itinerary. Shown arriving in Southampton for the first time on 3rd April 1995 where, three days later, HM The Queen named her with the traditional bottle of champagne, emphasising that, though German-built, ORIANA is very much a British ship in concept, design, decor and registration. Her Officers are British and her cosmopolitan crew includes a proportion of Goanese stewards in the P&O tradition.   (Photo: Carola Ingall)

ORIANA (II)

1995.   Cruise Liner

ORIANA leaving Southampton on her maiden cruise, accompanied by, so it seemed at the time, every small boat in the Solent area. Her "voice" boomed out over the waterfront bringing memories of the day I sailed from there on CANBERRA's maiden voyage as a member of her ship's Company. ORIANA's silhouette, satisfies my own idea of a ship. Visiting her before she sailed, I liked the atmosphere on board—I felt I could recognise the feel of a P&O ship. Her interior represents a blend of design illustrating the history, heritage and tradition of the Company, while supplying the most up to date facilities and comforts even the most demanding passenger could ask for.   (Photo: Carola Ingall)

SUN PRINCESS (II)

1995.   Cruise Liner

Built by Fincantieri at Monfalcone in Italy. Her three predecessors having been ordered by Sitmar, this ship is the first in the Princess Fleet since ROYAL PRINCESS to be built to the order of P&O. The designer, Norwegian Njal Eide, was asked to produce a ship with the ambience of a smaller vessel, while offering passengers all they have come to expect in a first class cruise liner such as two atriums with shops, lounges and bars, a computerised golf centre, more private balconies and a promenade deck which encircles the ship—evoking memories of "8 times round C Deck equals a mile". On entry into service, SUN PRINCESS qualified as the largest cruise liner in the world. Her passenger/space ratio is extremely generous compared with other similar sized vessels.

Sister ships: DAWN PRINCESS (II) (1996), SEA PRINCESS (II) (1999), OCEAN PRINCESS (2000).

GRAND PRINCESS
Due 1997. Cruise Liner
Ordered from Fincantieri at Monfalcone in Italy. At 105,000 tons, the largest cruise ship ever built. It is planned that she will carry 2,600 passengers, 80% of them in cabins with private balconies, the highest percentage so far in the Company. She will have a retractable magrodome over one of her swimming pools and a nightclub 15 decks up, as well as three show lounges, three main restaurants—truly a travelling "Grand Hotel"—what a long way from IBERIA, the first ship featured in this book.....

SELECT BIBLIOGRAPHY

BAILLIE, Captain D.G.O.: *"A Sea Affair"*, Hutchinson & Co (Publishers) Ltd, 1957

CABLE, Boyd: *"A Hundred Year History of the P&O"*, Ivor Nicholson & Watson, 1937.

COURSE, Captain A.G.: *"Ships of the P&O"*, Adlard Coles Ltd, 1954.

DIVINE, David: *"These Splendid Ships"*, Frederick Muller Ltd, London, 1960.

EMMONS, Frederick: *"Pacific Liners"*, David & Charles 1973.

HAWS, Duncan: *"Ships and the Sea: A Chronological Review"*, Hart-Davies MacGibbon Ltd 1976, Chancellor Press 1985; *"Merchant Fleets in Profile: The Ships of the P&O, Orient and Blue Anchor Lines"*, Patrick Stephens Ltd 1978

HOWARTH, David and HOWARTH, Stephen: *"The Story of P&O"*, Weidenfeld & Nicolson 1987, Updated edition 1994.

HOOK, F.A.: *"Merchant Adventurers"*, A. & C. Black Ltd 1920.

KENDALL, F.R.: *"Dearest Mother"*, Ed Brian Macdonald, Lloyds of London Press Ltd, 1988.

KLUDAS, Arnold: *"Great Passenger Ships of the World"*, Volumes 1–6, Patrick Stephens Ltd.

McCART, Neil: *"20th Century Passenger Ships of the P&O"*, Patrick Stephens Ltd, 1985. "Famous British Liners" Series: "ss VICEROY OF INDIA" 1993, "ARCADIA and IBERIA" 1993, "P&O's Five White Sisters" (The STRATHs) 1994, "P&O's CANBERRA and SEA PRINCESS" 1993, Fan Publications.

MUXWORTHY, Lt Cdr J.L. RN: *"CANBERRA The Great White Whale Goes to War"*, P&OSN Company, 1982.

NICOLSON, John: *"Arthur Anderson A Founder of the P&O Coy"*, Paisley: Alexander Gardner, 1914.

PADFIELD, Peter: *"Beneath the Houseflag of the P&O"*, Hutchinson & Co (Publishers) Ltd, 1981.

RABSON, Stephen & O'DONOGHUE, Kevin: *"P&O A Fleet History"*, World Ship Society, 1988.

RENTELL, Philip: *"Historic P&O-Orient Liners"*,, Kingfisher Publications, 1990.

SANKEY, Raymond:: *"Maritime Heritage: Barrow & Morecambe Bay"*, Silver Link Publishing Ltd 1986.

THACKERAY, William Makepeace: *"Notes of a Journey From Cornhill to Grand Cairo"* Introduction by Sarah Searight, Cockbird Press, 1991.

P&OSN Company: *"P&O In the Falklands"* 1982, "About Ourselves" Staff Journal, "Wavelength" Company Newspaper.

INDEX

1. Roman numerals following a ship's name indicate that she is the first, second, third etc, vessel to carry that name in the P&O fleet.

2. Dimensions are registered length × breadth × depth, except in cases where the overall length is quoted. For ease of reference all dimensions are rounded off to the nearest foot or metre. Metric measurements apply to vessels which entered the Company's service from 1979.

3. Gross tonnage is shown as completed or as rebuilt (see Note 7). It should be noted that these figures vary by subsequent modifications or changes to the measurement rules. It should be noted that these figures may vary by subsequent modifications or changes to the measurement rules.

4. Engine types are indicated as follows: Reciprocating: C = compound; T = triple expansion; Q = quadruple expansion; Turbine: Tur = steam turbine; Diesel: D = diesel; ihp: indicated horse power; shp: shaft horse power; bhp: brake horse power

5. Screws. The number of screws is shown thus: 1×S, 2×S etc.

6. Speed. The speed given in P&O specifications is quoted in knots.

7. Rebuilt. In the case of ships substantially modified during their careers, amended details appear immediately below their first entry.

	Dimensions	Tonnage	Machinery	Speed	Page
BALLARAT (I)	500 × 63 × 38	11120	2 Q 4c 2×S 9000 ihp	14	50
BARADINE (I)	520 × 64 × 38	13144	2 Q 4c 2×S 9500 ihp	13.5	67
BELTANA	500 × 62 × 38	11120	2 Q 4c 2×S 9000 ihp	14	51
BENALLA	500 × 62 × 30	11118	2 Q 4c 2×S 9000 ihp	14	52
BENDIGO (II)	527 × 69 × 43	8782	3 Tur 1×S 13000 shp	17	128
BORNEO	401 × 47 × 28	4573	T 3c 3500 ihp	13.5	16
CALEDONIA	486 × 54 × 26	7558	T 5c 11000 ihp	18	15
CANBERRA	819 × 103 × 33	45733	2 Turbo alt elec drive 2×S 85000 shp	27	136–138, 172
CANNANORE	465 × 63 × 28	7065	6c 2 SCSA 6800 bhp	15.5	120
CANTON (II)	349 × 42 × 27	3171	T 3c 2500 ihp	12	13
CANTON (III)	542 × 73 × 42	15784	6 Tur 2×S 18500 shp	18	104, 114
CARTHAGE (II)	523 × 71 × 33	14304	6 Tur 2×S 14000 shp	18	89–90
CATHAY (II)	524 × 70 × 42	15104	2 Q 4c 2×S 13437 ihp	16	74
CATHAY (III)	558 × 70 × 41	13809	2 Tur 1×S 9500 shp	17	134
CHINA (II)	501 × 54 × 25	7899	T 4c 11000 ihp	18	17
CHITRAL (I)	526 × 70 × 42	15248	2 Q 4c 2×S 13000 ihp	16	75–76
CHITRAL (II)	558 × 70 × 41	13821	2 Tur 1×S 9500 shp	17	135
CHUSAN (III)	647 × 85 × 36	24215	6 Tur 2×S 42500 shp	23	123–124
COMMONWEALTH	450 × 52 × 31	6616	2 T 3c 2×S 4000 ihp	13.5	47
COMORIN (I)	524 × 70 × 42	15116	2 Q 4c 2×S 13000 ihp	16	73
CORFU	523 × 71 × 33	14293	6 Tur 2×S 14000 shp	18	91
CROWN PRINCESS	m: 245 (inc BB) × 32 × 33	69845	4 D 2 elec motors 2×S 24000 kw	21.5	107, 159
DAWN PRINCESS (I)	m: 185 × 25 × 15	16666	4 Tur 2×S 24500 shp	19	154
DECCAN	368 × 43 × 30	3128	2c dir.act inv 2584 ihp	13.75	10
DONGOLA (I)	470 × 56 × 23	8038	2 Q 4c 2×S 8000 ihp	15.5	42
DONGOLA (II)	425 × 57 × 35	7371	T 3c 2250 ihp	9.5	118
EGYPT	500 × 54 × 25	7912	T 4c 11000 ihp	16	20
EMPIRE FOWEY As built	634 × 74 × 41	17526	Turbo elec 2×S 26000 shp	21	116–117
1950		19121	6 Tur 2×S 18000 shp	18	
EUXINE	223 × 29 × 19	1165	2 c dir.act osc 1070 ihp	12	3

	Dimensions	Tonnage	Machinery	Speed	Page
FAIR PRINCESS	m: 185 × 25 × 14	16627	4 Tur 2×S 24500 shp	19	153
FAIRSTAR	m: 186 × 24 × 17	21619	4 Tur 2×S 18000 shp	20	156
FORMOSA (I)	204 × 25 × 17	637	2c vert.act 800 ihp	8	5
GOLDEN PRINCESS	m: 205 × 25 × 14	28388	4 D 2×S 18000 bhp	18.5	161
GRAND PRINCESS	App. 105000 (No other statistics available as yet)				165
GREAT LIVERPOOL As built	214 × 26 × 19	1140	2c dir.act side lever 468 ihp	9	2
From 1840		1382			
HIMALAYA (I)	373 × 46 × 35	3438	2c horiz dir.act trunk 2050 ihp	13	7
HIMALAYA (II)	466 × 52 × 26	6898	T 3c 10000 ihp	18	14
HIMALAYA (III)	682 × 91 × 36	27955	6 Tur 2×S 42500 shp	22	105, 121–122
IBERIA (I)	155 × 24 × 15	516	2c Side lever 180 hp	9	1
IBERIA (II)	719 × 91 × 40	29614	6 Tur 2×S 42500 shp	22	132–133
INDIA (II)	500 × 54 × 25	7911	T 4c 11000 ihp	18	18–19
INDUS (I)	208 × 35 × 21	1386	2c dir.act osc 1367 ihp	10	4
1852	244 × 35 × 21	1951	1367 ihp		
ISIS	300 × 37 × 18	1728	2T 4c 2×S 6500 ihp	20	23
ISLAND PRINCESS	m: 169 (inc BB) × 25 × 15	19907	4 D 10c 4 SCSA 2×S 18000 bhp	19	142, 145
JEDFOREST	957 (inc BB) × 148 × 76	83714	8c SCSA 2 oil 30400 bhp	16.5	144
KAISAR-I-HIND (II)	520 × 61 × 33	11430	2 Q 4c 2×S 14000 ihp	18.5	56–57
KALYAN	480 × 58 × 34	8987	2 Q 4c 2×S 9000 ihp	15.5	58
KARMALA (I)	480 × 58 × 34	8983	2 Q 4c 2×S 9000 ihp	15	55
KASHMIR	480 × 58 × 34	8841	2 Q 4c 2×S 7000 ihp	14	59
KHIVA (II)	481 × 58 × 34	8947	2 Q 4c 2×S 7000 ihp	14	54
MACEDONIA	530 × 60 × 26	10512	2 Q 4c 2×S 13000 ihp	18	38–39
MALOJA (I)	550 × 63 × 34	12431	2 Q 4c 2×S 14000 ihp	19	48
MALOJA (II)	601 × 73 × 49	20837	2 Q 4c 2×S 13300 ihp	16	70–71
MALOJA (III)	559 × 72 × 39	12,763	2 Tur 1×S 8250 shp	14.5	139
MALWA (II)	540 × 61 × 25	10883	2 Q 4c 2×S 13000 ihp	18	45

	Dimensions	Tonnage	Machinery	Speed	Page
MANTUA (I)	540 × 61 × 25	10885	2 Q 4c 2×S 13000 ihp	16.5	46
MARMORA	530 × 60 × 26	10509	2 Q 4c 2×S 13000 ihp	17	36–37, 131
MEDINA	550 × 63 × 35	12350	2 Q 4c 2×S 14000 ihp	16.5	49
MOLDAVIA (I)	521 × 58 × 25	9500	2 T 3c 2×S 12000 ihp	16.5	32–33
MOLDAVIA (II)	552 × 72 × 38	16449	6 Tur 2×S 13250 shp	16	68
MONGOLIA (II)	521 × 58 × 25	9505	2 T 3c 2×S 12000 ihp	16.5	35
MONGOLIA (III)	552 × 72 × 39	16504	6 Tur 2×S 13000 shp	16	69
MOOLTAN (II)	520 × 58 × 25	9621	2 Q 4c 2×S 13000 ihp	18	40
MOOLTAN (III)	601 × 73 × 49	20847	2 Q 4c 2×S 13300 ihp	16	72
MOREA	540 × 61 × 25	10890	2 Q 4c 2×S 13000 ihp	16	44
NALDERA	581 × 67 × 44	15825	2 Q 4c 2×S 18000 ihp	17.5	61–63
NARKUNDA	581 × 69 × 28	16227	2 Q 4c 2×S 15300 ihp	17	62, 64–66
NELLORE	450 × 52 × 31	6853	2 Q 4c 2×S 4500 ihp	14	53
NYANZA (I)	327 × 36 × 28	2082	2 × 2c Osc 2304 ihp	12	9
OCEANA	468 × 52 × 27	6610	T 3c 7000 ihp	16.5	12
ORIANA (II)	m: 260 (inc BB) × 32 × 8	69253	4 D 2×S 32,000 bhp	24	
PACIFIC PRINCESS	m: 169 (inc BB) × 25 × 15	20636	4 D 10c 4 SCSA 2×S 18000 bhp	19	146–147
PATONGA	483 × 65 × 39	10071	3 Tur 1×S 9000 shp	15.5	127
PERSIA	500 × 54 × 25	7951	T 4c 11000 ihp	17	25–26, 39
PLASSY	450 × 54 × 32	7405	2 T 3c 2×S 6500 ihp	16	27
RAJPUTANA	548 × 71 × 43	16568	2 Q 4c 2×S 15000 ihp	17	84
RANCHI	549 × 71 × 43	16650	2 Q 4c 2×S 15000 ihp	17	80–82
RANPURA	548 × 71 × 43	16601	2 Q 4c 2×S 15000 ihp	16.5	78–79
RAWALPINDI	548 × 71 × 43	16619	2 Q 4c 2×S 15000 ihp	17	83
RAZMAK	500 × 63 × 34	10602	2 Q 4c 2×S 12000 ihp	18	77
REGAL PRINCESS	m: 245 (inc BB) × 32 × 34	69845	4 D 2 elec motors 2×S 24000 kw	21.5	160
ROYAL PRINCESS	m: 231 (inc BB) × 32 × 19	44348	4 D 6c 2×S 31543 bhp	21.5	151–152
SALSETTE (II)	440 × 53 × 20	5842	2 Q 4c 2×S 10000 ihp	20	43

	Dimensions	Tonnage	Machinery	Speed	Page
SEA PRINCESS (I) / VICTORIA (II)	m: 201 (inc BB) × 27 × 15	27670	2 9c 2 SCSA oil 2×S 25200 bhp	19.5	106, 148–150
SICILIA	450 × 52 × 30	6696	2 T 3c 2×S 4500 ihp	14	30
SINGAPORE (II)	499 × 69 × 30	9236	3 Tur 1×S 13000 shp	17	115, 125
SKY PRINCESS	m: 241 (inc BB) × 28 × 24	22120	4 Tur 2×S 29500 shp	19	155
SOCOTRA (II)	466 × 63 × 38	7840	2 4c 2 SCSA 2×S 9000 shp	16	115
SOMALI (I)	450 × 52 × 31	6708	2 T 3c 2×S 4500 shp	14	29
SOUDAN (I)	450 × 52 × 31	6680	2 T 3c 2×S 4500 ihp	14	28
SOUDAN (III)	502 × 67 × 32	9080	2 6c 2 SCSA 2×S 13600 bhp	17	119
SPIRIT OF LONDON /SUN PRINCESS (I)	536 (inc BB) × 82 × 54	17370	4 D 10c 4 SCSA 2×S 18000 bhp	19	142–143
STAR PRINCESS /ARCADIA (III)	m: 246 × 36 × 20	63524	4 D 2×S 52140 bhp	21.5	157–158
STRATHAIRD (I)	639 × 80 × 33	22544	2 Tur elec motors 2×S 28000 shp	21	95–97
STRATHALLAN	640 × 82 × 34	23722	6 Tur 2xs 24000 shp	21	112–113
STRATHCARRON	505 (inc BB) × 70 × 40	10031	6c 2 SCSA 11600 bhp	17	140
STRATHCONON	563 (inc BB) × 80 × 46	12539	9c 2 SCSA 20700 bhp	21	141
STRATHEDEN (I)	640 × 82 × 34	23722	6 Tur 2×S 24000 shp	20	110–111
STRATHMORE (I)	640 × 82 × 34	23428	6 Tur 2×S 24000 shp	20	98–100, 109
STRATHNAVER (I)	639 × 80 × 33	22547	2 Tur elec motors 2×S 28000 shp	21	92–94
SUNDA (III)	499 × 69 × 30	9235	3 Tur 1×S 13000 shp	17	126
SUN PRINCESS (I)	See SPIRIT OF LONDON				
SUN PRINCESS (II)	m: 261 × 32 × 57	77441	4 D 2 elec 2×S 62646 bhp	21.8	164
SYRIA (II)	450 × 52 × 31	6660	2 T 3c 2×S 4500 ihp	14	102
VECTIS (II)	230 × 30 × 17	751	2c osc 1058 ihp	13	6
VECTIS (III)	430 X 44 × 36	5010	4c C inv tandem 4677 ihp	14.5	101
1891	449 X 44 X 34	5545	T 4c 6000 ihp	16	
VICEROY OF INDIA	586 × 76 × 42	19648	2 Tur elec motors 2×S 17000 shp	19	85–87
VICTORIA (II)	See SEA PRINCESS (I)				

September 1997—CANBERRA bows out after 36 years of stalwart service.